Guide to Business Data Analytics

IIBA®
International Institute
of Business Analysis™

International Institute of Business Analysis, Toronto, Ontario, Canada.

ISBN (PDF): 978-1-927584-21-7

ISBN (eBook): 978-1-927584-22-4

ISBN (Print): 978-1-927584-20-0

Table of Contents

1 Introduction to Business Data Analytics

Most business decisions involve some degree of uncertainty and the decision-makers seldom know the exact outcome of their actions. Data plays a crucial and transformational role in how decision-makers view business uncertainties.

Data is a collection of unorganized facts or observations that can be processed to obtain valuable information. Analytics is the science of examining raw data and information in order to draw insights.

The volume of available data and the technical ability to quickly interpret insights from data are primary factors in reducing uncertainties in business decisions. Organizations are using data to improve their business processes and forecast typical business metrics, as well as support strategic decisions that shape their future.

Understanding and using business-relevant data is a means to obtain valuable insights to support more informed business decision-making. Organizations are investing in analytics initiatives to deliver on their strategic imperatives, innovate, and obtain competitive advantages in the marketplace. Such investments are driving the demand for skilled professionals with analysis and analytics knowledge and experience.

Data analysis impacts how businesses make decisions by:

- enabling new products and services and by creating new markets,
- disrupting existing markets and unseating secure businesses,
- driving increased efficiency (for example, for retailers to enable them to tailor products for customers),
- identifying growth opportunities,
- driving innovation,
- operating more efficiently,
- and improving risk management.

Business data analytics is an area of study that targets effective business decision-making as opposed to using the rigorous technical know-hows through which data is analyzed. Several business analysis tools, techniques, and competencies are used in business data analytics to direct analytics initiatives at many touch-points within the life cycle of an analytics initiative. This IIBA® Guide to Business Data Analytics emphasizes some of the significant business analysis and analytics concepts to build a foundational understanding that will guide practitioners through analytics initiatives.

Use of business data analytics for business decision-making is accomplished in the following ways:

- Asking foundational questions to shape strategic imperatives:
    - What will analytics initiatives and business data be used for?
    - How will insights from data drive business outcomes and value for the enterprise?
    - What type of business data is most likely to generate the insights needed?
    - What business problems are being addressed using business data analytics?
    - What is the hypothesis that will be tested?
    - What do the identified patterns from data inform us about the future?
- Highlighting how enterprise data is organized and managed:
    - What type of data is collected and captured?
    - What are the primary data sources for the enterprise (for example, customer, supplier, or product data)?
- How are we managing data quality?
    - What is the enterprise data strategy and architecture: legacy, data warehouse, data lakes and vaults, big data capable, and so forth?
- Understanding and communicating analytics results:
    - How can analytics results be best explained (for example, data coherence versus storytelling)?
    - How are analytics results presented to stakeholders visually?
    - What business inferences can be drawn out of the data?
- Integrating insights into initiatives:
    - Enterprise business processes
        - What business processes and workflows are impacted?
        - If the analytics results drive change, how will that change be managed?
        - How does an organization become more data sophisticated?
    - Technology
        - What IT systems need to be improved to capitalize on the insights?
        - Are any additional technology/systems required?
    - People
        - Is additional training needed in order to improve employee capabilities?

1.1 What is Business Data Analytics?

Business data analytics is a specific set of techniques, competencies, and practices applied to perform continuous exploration, investigation, and visualization of business data. The desired outcome of a business data analytics initiative is to obtain insights that can lead to improved decision-making. Business data analytics can be applied to investigate a proposed business decision, action, or a hypothesis, or to discover new insights from business data that may result in improved decision-making.

The business data analytics cycle is the iterative research process that seeks to answer a well-formed research question. Data analysis then explores the results of this research.

Business data analytics can be defined more specifically through several perspectives. These perspectives include, but are not limited to, business data analytics as a:

- movement,
- capability,
- data-centric activity set,
- decision-making paradigm, and
- set of practices and technologies.

1.1.1 Business Data Analytics as a Movement

Business data analytics as a movement involves a management philosophy or business culture of evidence-based problem identification and problem-solving. Evidence through data is the driver of business decisions and change. Rapid technological advances in the digitization of data and improved analytics methods are prompting businesses to adopt a data-driven management philosophy.

Example of Evidence-Based Problem Analysis in Insurance

For the insurance industry, generating better customer value has always meant getting a clearer picture of individual risk. By paying closer attention to the data people create daily, insurance companies can better anticipate needs, personalize offers, and tailor the customer experience. It is a shift from the practice of using demographics data to customize insurance products. Data such as telematics, social media, and lifestyle data can accurately reveal individual risk patterns through advanced analytics. The availability of such data has prompted insurers to change the way products are marketed and priced, and to better manage claims.

1.1.2 Business Data Analytics as a Capability

Business data analytics as a capability includes the competencies possessed by both the organization and its employees. Business data analytic competencies extend beyond those required to complete analytical activities, they include capabilities such as innovation, culture creation, and process design. This capability, or lack thereof, may define or constrict what the organization is capable of achieving through business data analytics.

Building Competencies for a Data-Driven Enterprise

Spotify is the largest on-demand streaming music provider in the world, with millions of users globally. As an experiment, Spotify wanted to send out a large number of emails that would tell customers if their friends have subscribed to the streaming service and the playlist they are listening to. The idea was to improve user engagement through by promoting it as a social experience. The initiative was a success. However, behind the scenes Spotify must have decided:

- what the data infrastructure for their organization should look like,
- how to source the relevant data about customers,
- how to design a solution that should be capable of sending out relevant email content,
- how to measure improved user engagement, and (above all)
- how to create a business case to justify the entire initiative.

The ability to perform advanced analytics on the data customers generate is definitely a part of the shift in approach. However, to operationalize such an initiative, the organization needs to treat data as an extension of organizational culture which translates into creative ideation, process change, and the agility required to embrace the changes brought in by a data-driven enterprise.

https://labs.spotify.com/2013/05/13/analytics-at-spotify/

1.1.3 Business Data Analytics as a Data-Centric Activity Set

Business data analytics as a data-centric activity set includes the actions required for an organization to use evidence-based problem identification and problem-solving. Data analytics has been defined by expert practitioners as involving six core data-centric activities:

- accessing,
- examining,
- aggregating,
- analyzing,
- interpreting, and
- presenting results.

Business data analytics, in addition to the core data-centric activities, extends the activity set to analysis-oriented activities:

- planning,
- strategy analysis,
- stakeholder collaboration and management,
- solution designing,
- recording and verifying analytics approaches, and
- tracking and managing analytics recommendations.

These activities are executed in a more structured way to help organizations realize the business objectives behind analytics initiatives.

1.1.4 Business Data Analytics as a Decision-Making Paradigm

Business data analytics as a decision-making paradigm involves making business data analytics a mechanism for informed decision-making across the organization. Business data analytics is the tool of making decisions using evidence-based problem identification and problem-solving. Evidence from data is an enabler for informed business decision-making that is more persuasive than instinctive decision-making which can be influenced by cognitive biases. Business data analysis strikes a balance between business experience and analytics results for effective business decisions through collaboration.

Examples of Collaborative Decision-Making

As deep analytics and artificial intelligence (AI) are becoming more prevalent in influencing decisions for enterprises, the underlying processes to arrive at a predictive or a prescriptive action are becoming more opaque. For example, the General Data Protection Regulation (GDPR) has provisions that give consumers the right to receive an explanation for any automated decision-making, such as the rate offered on a credit card or mortgage. The role of business data analytics becomes even more critical in this sense where evidence generated through data must be explained with the right business context to the decision-makers as well as end customers.

1.1.5 Business Data Analytics as a Set of Practices and Technologies

Business data analytics as a set of practices and technologies establishes the framework required to successfully execute analytics initiatives. These practices can be discussed in the context of six business data analytics domains:

- Identify the Research Questions,
- Source Data,
- Analyze Data,
- Interpret and Report Results,
- Use Results to Influence Business Decision-Making, and
- Guide Organizational-Level Strategy for Business Data Analytics.

These six business data analytics domains define the set of data-centric activities, as well as the business analysis practices that enable successful analytics initiatives.

1.2 The Business Data Analytics Cycle

The business data analytics cycle represents the research aspects of business analytics. It is an iterative cycle initiated through the development of a well-formed research question and then explored through targeted but thorough data analysis.

The cycle is based on the scientific method. The scientific method is a process for research that is used to explore observations and answer questions. The process starts by asking a question that scopes the research and is phrased as who, what, when, where, which, why, or how. Based on these questions, background information is collected and smaller scoped questions are formed. A question may take the following format:

If ________ happens then will ________ happen, or

Is __________ different to ___________, or

Does __________ affect ___________ etc.

The question is then tested using a method or procedure, and the results are analyzed to draw conclusions based on the smaller scoped question.

Business data analytics focuses on the data collection and data analysis part of the scientific method while the processes before and after this are informed by business analysis. Business data analytics requires business analysis to ensure the data analysis is focused on identifying questions that are of importance to answer and that the data produces valuable insights for resolving important business situations (problem or opportunity).

The scientific method paired with the business data analytics cycle:

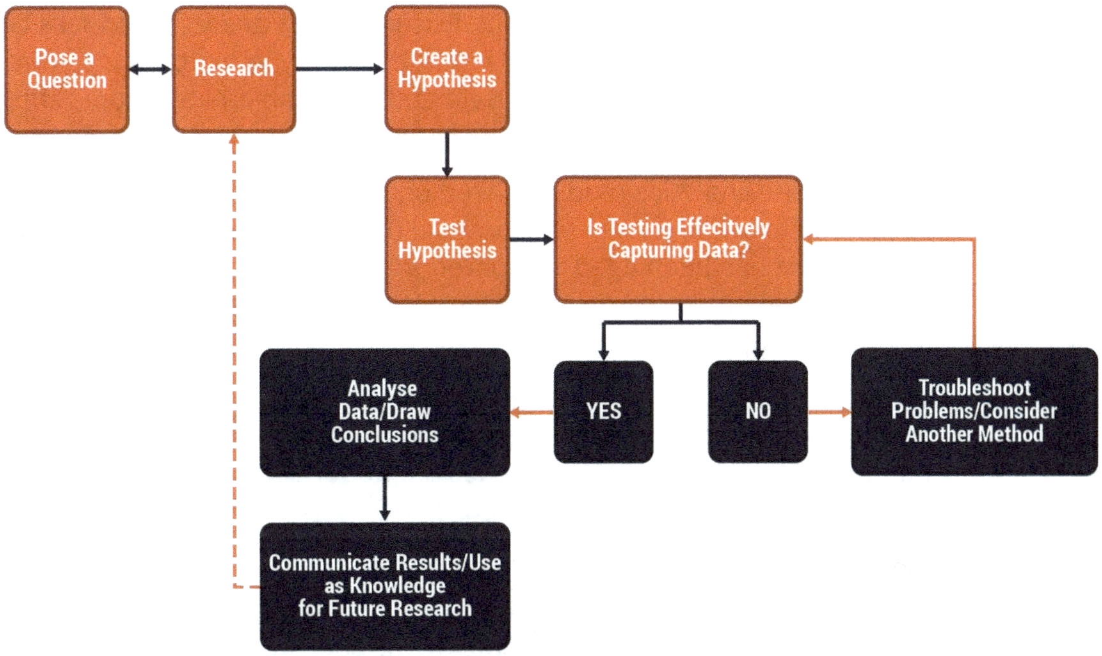

Taking an example where the organization is looking for a solution to address its employee turnover problem, the analytics cycle begins by posing a question such as "*How can we improve our staff retention rates?*"

After conducting initial research, it may be discovered that turnover is effected by several factors resulting in the need to create several hypotheses, one of which might be "*Does work overload affect turnover in our organization?*" The organization may develop a survey to measure work overload and turnover and administer it to current and past employees. The results of the survey may be analyzed to understand any cause and effect relationships. It might be determined that work overload is high in parts of the organization that have or are experiencing a large amount of turnover. These results may lead the organization to put measures in place to re-balance work or decrease the workload of individual employees or roles.

Despite its similarities to the scientific method, the business data analytics process has some slight differences. For one, the business data analytics process may differ depending on the type of analysis taking place. Testing may not always include an experiment to collect data, as the data might simply be accessed from a server using existing data sources. In business data analytics, it is necessary to perform data validation and verification on the data collected. In the scientific method, data validation may not be required because the data collected as part of a scientific experiment is obtained in a controlled environment.

When the objective of the analytics effort is continuous improvement or some other metric of improvement over time, the business analytics cycle is on-going and iterative.

In the context of projects, with defined end points, the conclusions drawn from a project may be used to form new research questions in-turn perpetuating another execution of the entire business data analytics cycle.

1.3 Business Data Analytics Objectives

Business decisions can easily be based on personal and individual experience, expertise, and instinct. Business data analytics reduces cognitive and personal biases by using data as the primary input for decision-making. When performed well, business data analytics can create a competitive advantage for the organization.

For example, analytics models based on weather, soil, and other conditions have been found to be more accurate in predicting the price and quality of red wine after it has been aged compared to the wine experts who influence the decision-making based on their own cognitive biases as to what they enjoy and do not enjoy in a wine.

The objective of business data analytics is to explore and investigate business problems or opportunities through a course of scientific inquiry. The specific outcomes of business data analytics are dependent on the type of analysis and inquiry that is being performed.

There are four types of analytics methods:

- ***Descriptive***: Provides insight into the past by describing or summarizing data. Descriptive analytics aims to answer the question "What has happened?"
  - Example: Aggregation and summarization of sales data based on geographic regions.
- ***Diagnostic***: Explores why an outcome occurred. Diagnostic analytics is used to answer the question "Why did a certain event occur?"
  - Example: Investigation of dipping revenue in a particular quarter.
- ***Predictive***: Analyzes past trends in data to provide future insights. Predictive analytics is used to answer the question "What is likely to happen?"
  - Example: Predicting profit or loss that is likely to happen in the next financial year.
- ***Prescriptive***: Uses the findings from different forms of analytics to quantify the anticipated effects and outcomes of decisions under consideration. Prescriptive analytics aims to answer the question "What should happen if we do ...?"
  - Example: What will happen to the total sales if the organization increases the marketing spend by 10%?

TIME/QUESTION TYPE	WHAT	WHY
PAST	**DESCRIPTIVE** What happened?	**DIAGNOSTIC** Why did it happen?
PAST/FUTURE	**PREDICTIVE** What is likely to happen based on past trends?	
FUTURE	**PRESCRIPTIVE** What should happen if we take a certain path? What is the best outcome given the uncertainty?	

New modelling techniques are now available due to the advances in machine learning, deep learning, optimizations, and advanced data science. These techniques, coupled with the availability of disparate data and related data infrastructure, have increased the feasibility of deploying analytics solutions for business problems or opportunities.

Examples of Analytics Contexts and Business Use Cases

Analytics Context	Typical Business Cases
Customer Analytics	• Predicting customer churn and behaviour • Understanding customer segments • Developing proactive campaigns to retain them • Understanding customer lifetime value
People Analytics	• Understanding and predicting attrition • Assessing performance
Supply Chain Analytics	• Predicting and matching demand and supply • Managing inventories • Conducting root cause and failure analysis
BFSI Analytics (Banking, Financial Services, Insurance)	• Quantifying portfolio risks and value at risk (VaR) • Detecting and preventing fraud by implementing credit risk models • Pricing products
Digital Analytics	• Utilizing platforms and channels • Assessing digital marketing and search engine optimization • Analyzing web and social media engagement statistics

Examples of Analytics Contexts and Business Use Cases

Analytics Context	Typical Business Cases
Healthcare Analytics	• Predicting disease vectors and outbreaks • Discovering new drugs and genomics • Researching for lifestyle diseases
Government and Public Sector Analytics	• Improving e-Governance initiatives • Understanding and acting on defense and security threats • Understanding public sentiment on policies

1.4 Business Analysis and Business Data Analytics

As data and analytics disciplines, such as business intelligence, data analysis, data science, and business analytics, evolved they have all leveraged business analysis practices. However, significant differences exist between business analysis and analytics disciplines in terms of objective and overall approach.

Business Analysis

- Business analysis is the practice of enabling change in an enterprise by defining needs and recommending solutions that deliver value to stakeholders.
- Business analysis tools, techniques, and competencies can elevate the analytics initiatives to be more effective by providing the business context for analytics effort.
- Business analysis defines the focus for the analytics problem and sets the scope throughout the analytics initiative.
- Business analysis also aids in the collection of data and the implementation of the data collection processes.
- Business analysis activities are performed to communicate the results and facilitate the implementation of informed business decisions made as a result of what is learned from analyzing the data collected.

Analytics Disciplines

- Analytics disciplines focus primarily on data analysis in a systematic process to observe and predict trends and patterns.
- Typical practices and procedures in data analytics are used to sort, process, and analyze the data once assembled which is aided by business analysis.
- Once the analysis of the collected data is complete, business analysis activities are performed to interpret the results obtained from data analytics and transform information into business decisions.

Some consider data analytics as a specialty or subset of business analysis; one that is focused on data analysis. This viewpoint is taken since many skills and competencies often discussed when performing business analysis are equally applicable when performing data analytics work.

Here we treat business analysis and data analytics disciplines separately. We identify business data analytics as a specialized area of study that contains aspects of business analysis and analytics disciplines and is used for creating better business outcomes through evidence-driven business decisions. The business analysis and analytics concepts discussed here are useful to both business analysis and analytics professionals alike to generate value for the enterprise through analytics initiatives.

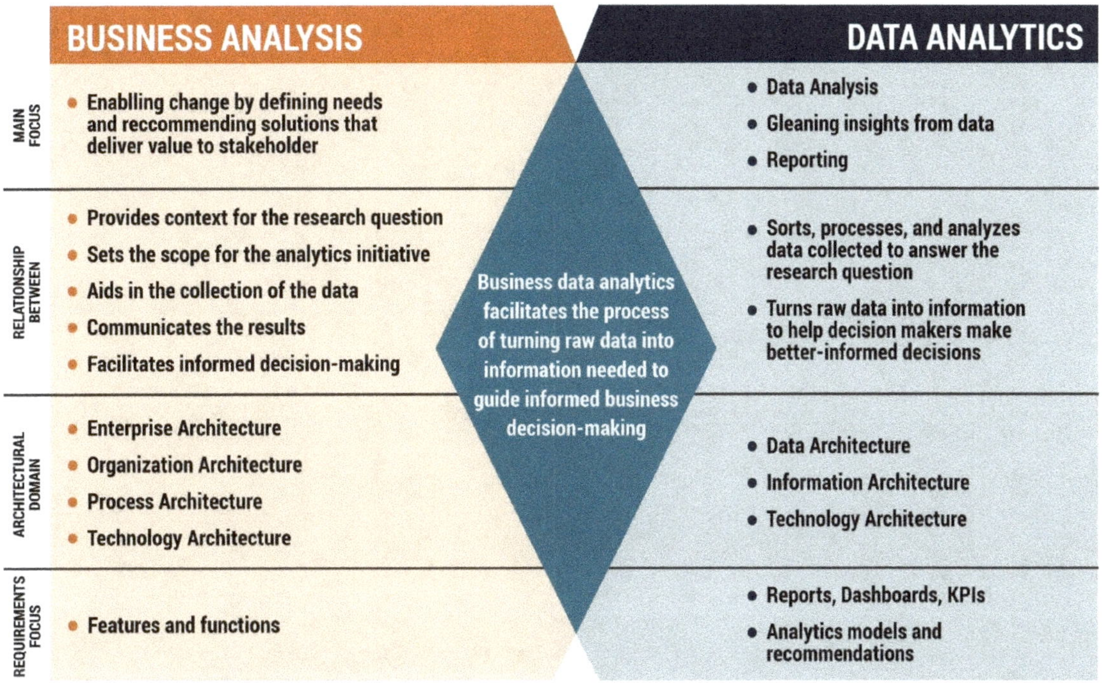

2 Business Data Analytics Domains and Tasks

Business Data Analytics Domains and Tasks presents the practices and activities that are commonly considered business data analytics work. Emphasis is placed on identifying areas where business analysis skills are important to perform the business data analytics tasks and not on identifying the job title that would take responsibility for performing the work.

Business data analytics responsibilities can be assigned in a variety of ways and should be delegated to the resources having the best skill set to complete the work, regardless of their job title. While many of the tasks can be performed by those with the title business analyst, on an analytics initiative, anyone with business analysis skills from business analysts, data analysts, data scientists, business architects, and business subject matter experts (SMEs) may complete the work.

The tasks are grouped and presented in the context of six business data analytics domains:

- 2.1 Identify the Research Questions,
- 2.2 Source Data,
- 2.3 Analyze Data,
- 2.4 Interpret and Report Results,
- 2.5 Use Results to Influence Business Decision-Making, and
- 2.6 Guide Organizational-Level Strategy for Business Data Analytics.

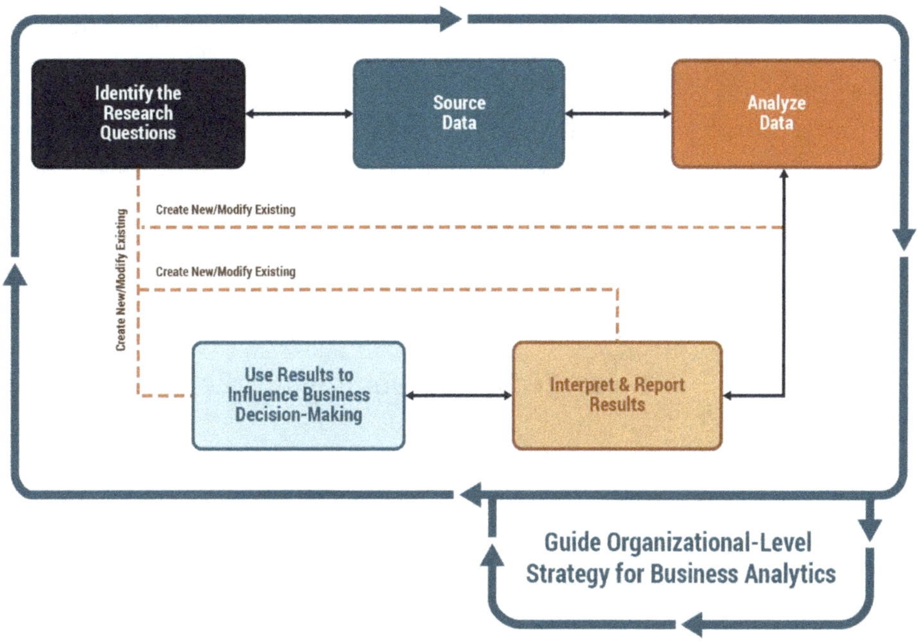

2.1 Identify the Research Questions

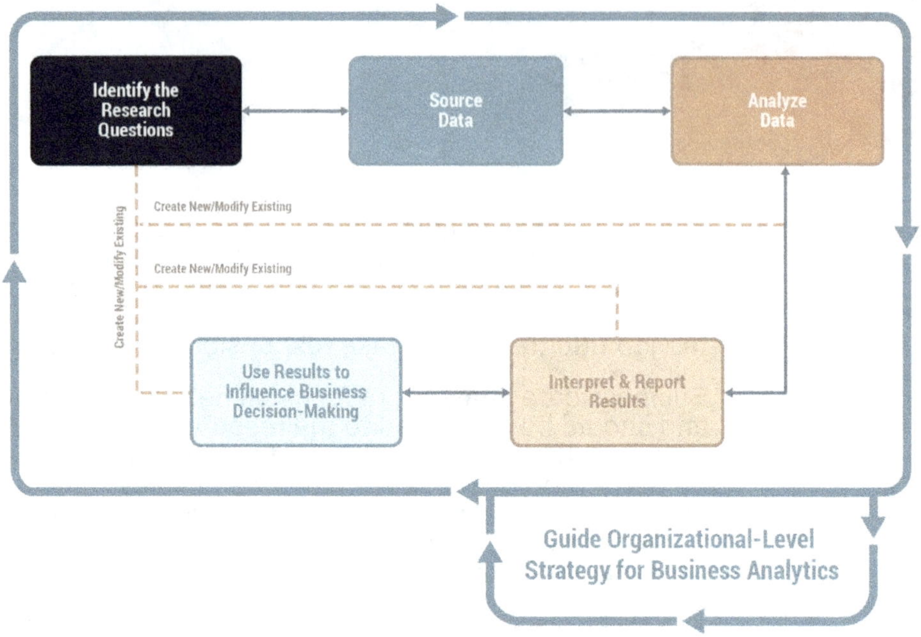

Most stakeholders can instinctively identify the symptoms of a business problem based on their expertise and knowledge of business processes, rules, and practices. To investigate these problems or opportunities and produce outcomes that are aligned to business goals, a structured approach to identifying research questions is required.

The research questions provide focus for the data analytics team and shape the work that follows. The goal is to use the subsequent data analysis to generate insights to support more informed business decision-making.

Tasks in the Identify the Research Questions domain include:

- Define Business Problem or Opportunity.
- Identify and Understand the Stakeholders,
- Assess Current State,
- Define Future State,
- Formulate Research Questions,
- Plan Business Data Analytics Approach, and
- Select Techniques for Identify the Research Questions.

2.1.1 Define Business Problem or Opportunity

Although the tasks in business data analytics are iterative and not sequential, defining the business problem or opportunity is often the first step performed in any business data analytics initiative. This task is where those with strong business analysis skills can assist with the work.

Often, when analytics engagements start, the task of identifying a problem is not given enough attention or the right stakeholders are not identified. There is often an urgency to see results from the investment in analytic initiatives. This can create a tendency to jump into a solution focus rather than devote enough attention to identifying to problem and engaging the right stakeholders. This can lead to problems not being analyzed in sufficient detail and resulting in a misdiagnosis of the business problem.

Business data analytics involves analysts performing business problem discovery in parallel with the task of identifying and understanding the right stakeholders. An analyst may facilitate discussions with stakeholders to elicit, observe, and analyze through a process of continuous discovery of any and all relevant information that will help the team understand the context of the situation.

Sometimes the organization is experiencing a problem that business data analytics can help solve, such as understanding why there is a sudden decrease in internet sales. In other situations, the organization may be interested in using business data analytics to uncover opportunities—as in the case of a manufacturing company looking to collect maintenance and performance data on its machinery to determine how to predict and avoid equipment outages. In either scenario, analysts use various business analysis elicitation and problem analysis techniques to obtain the necessary information required to define the business problem or opportunity that analytics might address.

It is important to note the outcome of this Define Business Problem or Opportunity involves identifying the business problem that may lead to one or more research questions/problems. Then, further analysis is conducted to formulate the right analytics questions from the business problem or opportunity under consideration.

Business problem or opportunity is usually a higher-level description than a research question/problem.

When defining the business problem or opportunity, analysts use several elicitation techniques such as interviews, job shadowing, surveys, and workshops. Business and organizational knowledge are useful when facilitating discussions.

2.1.2 Identify and Understand the Stakeholders

Identifying and understanding stakeholders allows analysts to actively engage and collaborate with the variety of stakeholders involved in an analytics initiative. Each stakeholder group:

- articulates different needs and objectives,
- poses different types of research questions,
- is interested in different volumes and timings of analytics results,
- holds different skillsets for interpreting those results, and
- possesses different levels of education in, and experience with, analytics.

Understanding the unique characteristics of each stakeholder group increases the analysts' effectiveness with each group. Before an initiative starts, analysts seek to answer the following questions:

- Who are the stakeholders?
- What is their level of knowledge about analytics?
- What aspect of the project is of interest to them?
- What communication methods and techniques are appropriate?
- When should stakeholders be communicated to?

It is critical to understand the custodians and consumers of data to identify the relevant stakeholders for an analytics initiative.

When identifying and understanding stakeholders, analysts use techniques such as brainstorming, interviews, or reviewing process flows and organizational charts.

In an analytics initiative, it is critical to have a data view of the business problem where analysts try to understand who:

- is creating the relevant information,
- is exposed to the data created within the organization, and
- are the decision-makers being influenced by the insights derived from the data.

Analysts use models such as stakeholder matrices and onion diagrams to depict aspects of their stakeholders. Analysts also create models to show how the organization's strategic goals relate to the organizational goals and objectives and the stakeholders or stakeholder groups impacted. They create or review personas to gain a deeper understanding of stakeholders. Facilitation and communication skills, along with knowledge about the business or specific organizations, help analysts perform stakeholder identification.

2.1.3 Assess Current State

Business data analytics is used to enable organizations to make informed decisions. Understanding the current state of the organization or context of the proposed change is fundamental to informed decision-making. Information obtained from a current state assessment provides important context so that the results of data analysis can be better interpreted.

Analyzing the current state involves understanding the business need and how it relates to the way the organization currently functions. The results of the current state analysis set a baseline and context for making a change. Whether discussing the changes associated with the implementation of a new customer relationship management (CRM) system or the process changes proposed after gaining insightful information from the results of a business data analytics effort, analyzing the current state is an important task.

A current state assessment can include understanding the business value chain or how data and information flow throughout the organization. From a data analytics perspective, the analysis of the current state involves determining what the existing data is pointing towards. This can be in the form of insights gained from previous analytics engagements or through the exploration of existing data using statistical or mathematical models or intuitions.

Conducting a current state assessment involves understanding organizational capabilities, resources, and business processes, in order to fully understand the business problem and derive research questions from it. All the tools, techniques, and models used are evidence-driven. For example, a business leader simply stating that there has been a reduction of internet sales due to lack of customer engagement does not conclusively link reduced sales to low customer engagement. Analysts look for concrete evidence from data and analysis to substantiate that hypothesis.

The analyst may uncover insights such as whether the organization has an appetite for analytics, the budget, and the expertise to perform the work. They necessarily become knowledgeable in the business domain and understand trends and evolving business models.

When conducting a current state assessment, analysts use business model canvas, organizational, scope, and process modelling to elicit, analyze, and visually depict the current state of the organization. Conceptual and systems thinking, along with business acumen and solution knowledge, help analysts understand and communicate the current state.

Example of Current State Analysis to Refine Research Questions

Using current state analysis to refine research questions can be demonstrated by reviewing some challenges of forecasting for a typical newsvendor problem.

A family-owned company that specialize in making world-class bicycles and parts has gone through a recent leadership change. Like many organizations that conduct a yearly forecast, the new leader is also faced with the most critical aspect of the job—forecasting and committing to fulfilling the total product demand, thereby determining a significant share of the next year's success. Forecasting was a pressing issue as the product portfolios had continued to grow even as product life cycles, along with customer patience regarding delivery, were becoming shorter. As always, the company's order commitment to its suppliers had to be made six months before the start of the season in September, without having any early indication of demand. The new leader wanted to adopt in new best practices, knowledge, and processes that included new ways of forecasting the demand.

In this case, the business need is to accurately forecast the demand for the products ahead of time, which corresponds to a research question on discovering the factors that influence the forecast. The accuracy of the forecast would determine the strategy for the company for the entire year and impact decisions across the value chain such as procurement, logistics, and marketing. A current state analysis, in the data context, usually involves the study of the business model, supply-chain analysis, analysis of the existing forecasting process, and analysis of the utility of the data available for forecasting. The analysis may reveal many constraints, insights, and assumptions that affect the nature of the research question.

If the current state analysis was not performed, the research question would only involve assessing the current forecasting model. An accurate current state analysis may reveal that the business model could be revised. Instead of using the same supplier for procuring bicycle parts, different local suppliers could be used, and the bicycles could be assembled locally. This would change the current research question from trying to improve the forecasting model to researching the factors that would maintain the quality, pricing, and sales.

Similarly, if the current state analysis of historical data revealed a clear trend of seasonal demand during longer holidays, the research question would involve a study of seasonal patterns that could be used to upgrade the forecasting model. These two examples, a change in the business model, or a change in the forecasting approach, are clear results of current state analysis that refine the original research problem to new or re-framed research problems that are more relevant.

2.1.4 Define Future State

Defining the future state creates a vision of the desired outcome of the change. Defining success for a business data analytics initiative is as important as any other change initiative. Defining the future state includes ensuring:

- the future state is clearly defined and understandable,
- that it is achievable with the resources available,
- that key stakeholders have a shared vision, developed by consensus of the outcome being sought, and
- measurable objectives are established to ensure the desired vision is met.

According to *A Guide to the Business Analysis Body of Knowledge® (BABOK® Guide)* version 3, purposeful change includes a definition of success.

To establish measurable objectives, analysts facilitate discussions between stakeholders to determine the types of metrics to consider. Working collaboratively, decision-makers select the most appropriate measures to assess using business data analytics. These measures may be a combination of strategic and operational key performance indicators (KPIs). Some KPIs may focus on assessing performance for a specific geography or a target audience. There may be industry-specific metrics such as average revenue per user (ARPU), which is used in telecom, or "store footfall" which is used in retail to count customers visiting the store.

Another important aspect of defining the future state is establishing the scope for the analytics effort. Establishing the scope involves understanding which areas of the organization are participating in the analytics effort and determining what stakeholders have questions to raise and information to provide.

A future state, concerning an analytics initiative, could also include setting a vision about the length and breadth of analytics capabilities. For example, tracking more KPIs, increasing the frequency of reports being generated from monthly to daily/weekly, automating reporting functionality, or having data available in real-time. Apart from descriptive objectives like tracking KPIs on the past data, predictive and prescriptive analytics may involve certain anticipated changes to business processes that drive multiple change initiatives.

The future state of an analytics initiative evolves throughout the life cycle of the engagement. Analysts manage and record the changes to future state.

Given the potential evolution of the vision, analysts are challenged in describing the changes reflected in the current understanding of the future state. Like most other activities in an analytics initiative, defining the future state is continuous and iterative.

The desired output from defining the future state is a clear understanding of the business objectives and the value the business is seeking to obtain from the analytics effort.

Analysts use metrics, KPIs, and different models to visually communicate the future state. This includes scope models to understand boundaries and stakeholder maps to identify those who might be impacted by this work.

Conceptual thinking skills help analysts understand the big picture and provide the context for the analytics work. Interaction skills, communication skills, analytical thinking, and problem-solving skills are useful when leading discussions to identify metrics and establish objectives.

Real-World problem in Defining the Future State for a Predictive Classification Problem

Detecting fraud is a perennial problem in multiple industries such as banking, finance, insurance, and telecom. It is a typical use case in analytics called binary classification. That is simply saying a particular transaction based on the analytics model is classified as fraud or not. For such a problem, the measure of success is governed by the business context and the identified business problem which the analysts formulate while defining the future state. There are some standard measures such as precision, recall, specificity, or accuracy that are commonly used for such types of problems described by the following formulas:

$Precision = TP/(TP+FP)$, $Recall = TP/(TP+FN)$,

$Specificity=TN/(FP+TN)$, $Accuracy=(TP+TN)/(TP+FP+TN+FN)$

Where,

TP = True Positive. The number of transactions predicted as fraud which are actually fraudulent.

FP = False Positive. The number of transactions predicted as fraud but are not fraudulent.

TN= True Negative. The number of transactions predicted as not fraud and are not actually fraudulent.

FN = False Negative. The number of transactions predicted as not fraud but are actually fraudulent.

Consider a scenario where a business wants to detect fraudulent transactions for credit cards. There are many factors (transaction time, location, and amount) which influence a transaction to be classified as fraudulent. When this type of fraud is detected algorithmically, there is a possibility that many transactions will be misclassified. A transaction may be predicted as fraud but in reality, it may be a valid transaction (a false positive). Similarly, a transaction can also be misclassified as a false negative. Depending on what the business wants to achieve, the criteria of success for the fraud detection analytics model may change. If the business wants to detect as much fraud as possible, the analytics model is adjusted so that the maximum number of true positives are detected. But, this also increases the chances of false positives. If the business stakeholders take a conscious decision that false positives are not a concern then the analytics model may only focus on precision as the most appropriate metric to maximize.

On the other hand, the business may want to define success as a measure of the actual cost to the company. The actual cost would be a trade-off between cost saved by predicting fraudulent transactions versus cost incurred for incorrectly predicting a fraud (cost of false positives and false negatives). In this case, precision will not be the right metric to pursue.

The key takeaway for analysts from this discussion is depending upon the business context the success criteria of an analytics initiative changes. The analyst must be able to articulate business context to the analytics team and similarly, explain to the business stakeholders any mathematically complex measure in simple business terms.

2.1.5 Formulate Research Questions

Before any of the detailed analytics work is performed, the stakeholders formulate the question that the analytics will answer. The research inquiries are derived from the business needs. The business need is problem or opportunity of strategic or tactical importance to be addressed.

For example, if the business need is to improve the customer experience of a retail store, the questions will be:

1. What are the factors that influence customer experience? (Descriptive analytics)
2. What are the measures for evaluating customer experience? (Descriptive analytics)
3. How do you classify individual transactions on the retail side as a positive or negative experience? (Predictive analytics)
4. Will customer experience improve by adding a new feature such as a pay wallet? (Prescriptive analytics)

Business needs can lead to different solutions and approaches which may or may not involve analytics initiatives. One or more of the analytics problems or opportunities may lead to one or more analytics initiatives where the research questions are further refined until they can be identified using a measurable success standard.

Formulating the research question involves facilitating discussions to identify the different problems to be explored, specifying the questions in an easily understood language, and bringing the team to a consensus as to the best set of analytics questions to answer.

Analysts require the skills to identify the right problem or opportunity and to focus the team on the right question to ensure the analytics work is guided properly. Discussions move beyond brainstorming a list of ideas to producing a concrete list of specific analytics questions the team believes are worth pursuing. On occasion, the team may need to identify what data are available before determining which ideas are achievable with analytics. The question, once formed, guides the scope and drives the activities of the analytics team.

The results of the analysis obtained when defining the business problem or opportunity, analyzing the current state, and defining the future state provides context when formulating the analytics questions. The analytics team, including business stakeholders, may start with a long list of questions and require ongoing collaboration to reduce the list identifying the highest valued questions to use. Technical resources or the analyst, based on their understanding of the data and the business problem or opportunity, may suggest an analytics problem that could be explored.

Good analytics questions are clearly stated and do not use technical language. The questions are reviewed with all stakeholders to ensure consensus that clearly articulates what the organization is looking to answer through analytics. In the Perform Data Analysis task (for more information,

see 2.3.4 Perform Data Analysis), the data scientist/analytics experts restate the analytics questions using more mathematical language.

There are situations where it is more efficient for an analytics team to address a group of questions for multiple initiatives, rather than individual initiatives asking one question at a time.

When formulating research questions, analysts utilize a variety of elicitation techniques to facilitate discussions with stakeholders, decision models to help the team reach consensus, and templates to guide the development of the question. Strong facilitation, leadership and negotiation skills are useful when facilitating consensus among stakeholders.

2.1.6 Plan Business Data Analytics Approach

Planning the Business Data Analytics Approach defines how analytics work will be performed. When planning a business data analytics approach, analysts:

- determine the capabilities and capacity of the organization to perform analytics so the team understands what is realistically possible,
- identify “quick wins” versus longer-term efforts,
- determine the type of analytics questions being asked for (descriptive, diagnostic, predictive, or prescriptive), and
- maintain traceability of business needs, objectives, research questions, and their sources (for example, stakeholders who asked the research questions or analysis that pointed to specific research questions).

Planning is an iterative process and changes to the approach are made as new knowledge is gained. Each of the six business data analytics domains includes an element of planning which may influence the overall approach to analytics.

There is no right or wrong answer as to the degree of formality of the business data analytics approach. Some organizations may choose to formally document the decisions made when defining their approach by using a business data analytics planning template. Other teams may choose to build more visual models to capture the decisions and include the information on shared wikis and within the team's workspace.

When planning the business data analytics approach, analysts use techniques such as brainstorming to quickly identify a list of activities needed to be performed, functional decomposition to break down high-level concepts into lower-level tasks, and estimation to assess how long it may take to complete various activities. Analysts planning the business data analytics approach use facilitation, leadership skills, and negotiation skills to obtain stakeholder consensus.

Planning Business Data Analytics Approach at Various Stages

When research questions or the solution approaches involve more complexity than anticipated, analytics initiatives are typically implemented in multiple stages of maturity:

- A proof of concept stage which focuses primarily on feasibility of the analytics approach.
- A pilot stage which focuses on limited scale solution to discover integration and quality issues.
- A production stage which focuses on business value for customers or internal stakeholders.

Deployment Stage	Level of Formality	Assessment of Organizational Capabilities and Resources	Planning Outlook	Data Characteristics
Proof of Concept	Low	• Qualitative assessment of capabilities • Independent and agile teams • Low governance • Only key stakeholder engagement • Flexible solution and data architecture	Near-term	• Static and limited data without data pipelines from different sources • Noisy but consciously curated
Pilot	Medium	• Both qualitative and measurable assessment • Larger teams with cross-functional capabilities • Some governance structure defined • Most stakeholders are identified and engaged • Solution and data architecture are defined	Mid- to long-term	• Dynamic data integrated to most of the known data sources • Usable data with defined transformation procedures
Production	High	• Both qualitative and measurable assessment • Larger teams with cross-functional capabilities • Governance structure deployed • Most stakeholders are identified and engaged • Solution and data architecture are implemented and integrated to enterprise architecture and data strategy and governance	Long-term	• Dynamic data integrated to most of the known data sources • Usable data with defined transformation procedures

2.1.7 Select Techniques for Identify the Research Questions

The following is a selection of some commonly used analysis and analytics techniques applicable to the Identify the Research Questions domain. The list of techniques does not represent a comprehensive set of techniques used by an analyst in the Identify the Research Questions domain but presents a small, but useful, set of techniques that can be used.

Techniques	Usage Context for Business Data Analytics	*BABOK® Guide* v3.0 Reference
Business Model Canvas	Used to understand how the enterprise produces value by analyzing the key component and business eco-system. It can be modified to include a data view on how data is used by the enterprise at a high level.	Chapter 10.8
Concept Modelling	Used to organize business vocabulary and their interrelationships. This can be used as a starting point to identify and validate data requirements as well as to correlate a business need for research questions.	Chapter 10.11
Decision Modelling and Analysis	Used to establish a decision hierarchy by capturing the flow of decisions that are commonly undertaken in an organization using various tools such as decision trees, tables, decision networks.	Chapters 10.16 and 10.17
Document Analysis	Used to understand the context through minutes of business meetings, internal reports, reports from other organizations, academic literature, previous analytics project reports, the data and methodology employed, the statistical results, and the subsequent business decisions.	Chapter 10.18
Interviews and Workshops	Used to understand the business problem or opportunity from the perspective of different stakeholders, or the organization as a whole, and to elicit more concrete research questions that contribute to the business problem or opportunity.	Chapters 10.25 and 10.50
Metrics and Key Performance Indicators (KPIs)	Used to measure the performance of the organization in different functional area or business goals. Many analytics engagements are undertaken to optimize or explain the KPIs and metrics.	Chapter 10.28
Organizational Modelling	Used to understand the organization's capabilities, resources, and group structures to discover levels of data insights and research questions posed by different groups in the context of their roles and capabilities.	Chapter 10.32
Prioritization	Used throughout the business data analytics effort to focus attention on the most urgent items. For example, when determining what is important to resolve, formulating research questions, sharing insights, and recommending actions.	Chapter 10.33

Techniques	**Usage Context for Business Data Analytics**	***BABOK® Guide* v3.0 Reference**
Process Modelling and Analysis	Used to understand the organization's processes where data is generated, and consumed, and to discover ways to identify improvement opportunities where analytics solutions may improve the business value.	Chapters 10.34 and 10.35
Risk Analysis and Management	Used to identify and manage any risks originating from a specific course of action, decision, or assumption that affect analytics engagement.	Chapter 10.38
Root Cause Analysis	Used to understand the business problem by systematically examining the probable causes to develop an intuition for the nature of research questions.	Chapter 10.40
Scope Modelling	Used to understand the scope and boundaries of the analytics engagement and the external context within which a future analytical solution may operate.	Chapter 10.41
Stakeholder List, Map, or Personas	Used to understand stakeholders and their characteristics with additional focus on how they generate and consume data and insights.	Chapter 10.43
Exploratory Data Analysis	Used to quickly understand the readily available data and insights to build intuition about the analytics problem and any contributing factors.	N/A
Hypotheses Formulation and Testing	Used to develop a premise for a particular result based on business stakeholder or SME's opinion which is statistically justified through the data to formulate research questions accurately.	N/A
Problem Reframing and Shaping	Used to facilitate deliberate thinking about a specific business or research problem from multiple perspectives such as stakeholder, market, or customer. Problems are restated for an analytics initiative. For example, if the analytics problem relates to identifying high-value customers of an organization for a custom marketing campaign, understanding what high-value means and reframing the problem. In this case, it may mean lifetime value, highest spending, or customers interested in high-value purchases.	N/A

2.1.8 A Case Study for Identify the Research Questions

.1 The Challenge

Marsha has worked as a business technology consultant at a large investment bank for the last four years. In that time, she has worked on several high-profile engagements and has forged strong working relationships with several key bank employees. John, one of the trading floor managers in the Chicago office, recently attended a big data conference and learned about some new approaches for leveraging predictive analytics tools on the trading floor.

John was convinced that his team would benefit from more sophisticated application of technology and analytics tools. He also worked with Marsha previously to establish and automate various types of trading floor transactions, and he knew Marsha was the ideal person to help with this work. John connected with Marsha and they discussed opportunities to help improve his team's efficiency using some of the newer approaches. After a conference call with Marsha and her consulting manager, John realized there were a number of outstanding issues that needed to be addressed before implementing any new tools. He also realized careful analysis of data would help identify the best way to move forward. John assured Marsha that any information, trading data, resources, and support from his team would be made available as she needed.

.2 Approach for Analyzing the Business Problem

As a seasoned professional, Marsha knows that seemingly simple business problems or opportunities often hide layers of complexity. She has seen the results of poorly conceived data analytics initiatives and knows that various key stakeholders have differing views of potential solutions. She also understands the need for developing a shared understanding of the business problem that needs to be solved as a crucial first step.

Marsha asked that they pause and take some time to develop a shared understanding of the problems to be addressed through application of new technology. Although John was eager to move quickly, he agreed to follow Marsha's recommendation of conducting a discovery workshop to fully understand the problems and prioritize the ones to be solved by use of analytics. Marsha proposed the following approach:

Workshop Stages	Workshop Planning and Activities
Pre-Workshop prep	• Identify relevant stakeholders using her experience with the bank and include John's suggestions for additional stakeholders. • Conduct initial research to develop relevant knowledge on pricing, market volatility assessment, and how trades are conducted on the trading floors. • Coordinate workshop logistics with John and develop the workshop agenda.
Workshop plan	• Highlight some of the key areas in investment banking where deep and non-traditional analytics approaches are being successfully used. John expects that it may be a big change for many of the stakeholders to consider new ways to conduct trades. He wants to provide a short explanation on the use of deep analytics. • Present some of her high-level research on the topic such as an industry point of view, benchmarking results, and competitive analysis. • Use analysis techniques such as root cause analysis, 5 Whys, and business model canvas to identify problems to be addressed. • Concretely define the business problems framed as research questions that data can help solve and outline the next steps.
Post-Workshop wrap-up	• Share the list of research questions and other workshop results with attendees. • Highlight next steps and follow up on the action items that may set the direction of future scoping and elicitation activities.

Pre-Workshop Activities

Based on her experience with the bank, Marsha assembled her initial list of stakeholders which included stakeholders from the Quantitative Research and Analysis team (Quants team) and the office of the Risk Management team (Risk team). John added additional stakeholders from his trading teams, operations, IT, and corporate governance. After agreeing on the workshop participants, agenda, and logistics, Marsha started her research work in preparation for the workshop.

Marsha conducted one-on-one interviews with John and some of the traders to learn about the business of trading desks. She learned how trade call sheets are communicated and how trades are executed on the trading floor, and created process models to capture this information.

She learned trade calls are passed to the traders by the Quants team who have modelled a complex process of predicting option price paths with a combination strategy using Black Scholes and RiskMetrics™ models. She saw that trades are divided into various groups such as speculations, hedges, and arbitrage teams. Marsha also learned how the Risk team sets daily Value at Risk (VaRs) based on traders' book, experience, and prior positions. She followed the process through, noting these parameters and trade plans are fed into the trading terminal at the trading desk. Although aware of the basics of these practices, Marsha realized she would need to understand additional process complexity to help the team discuss alternate sources of information for traders to consume. She decided to leave those discussions for the workshop.

The Discovery Workshop

The workshop started well as Marsha discussed how analytics models can be used in investment banking use cases. However, she felt uneasy with some of the comments. After asking some additional questions, it became apparent that both the Quants team and the Risk team were reluctant to provide their support. The Quants team members felt their predictive models were already cutting-edge and comparable to industry benchmarks. The Risk team were concerned the VaR computation would be impacted by the introduction of new models and significantly impact todays widely used processes. Marsha was able to redirect the participants to the benefits, including potential bottom line improvements that could occur. She was also able to leverage her research to demonstrate how competitors had addressed similar challenges. Both teams agreed it was important to proceed even if it meant changes to current practices.

With everyone on the same page, Marsha tackled the primary workshop objective which was to identify problems which could be answered through use of data analytics.

Post WorkShop Wrap-up

Marsha was able to consolidate the findings from the workshop and shared these with the group of stakeholders for agreement. By re-framing the business problem successfully, Marsha was able to demonstrate aspects that can be solved through business data analytics, as well as opportunities for both process and application development improvements. Marsha was able to share this outcome with the team and scheduled a follow-up discussion to prioritize these goals with John and other relevant stakeholders.

.3 Outcomes Achieved

Marsha leveraged her facilitation skills to drive the attendees towards a shared understanding and agreement about next steps. To get there, Marsha used specific business data analytics techniques to achieve incremental agreement, as follows:

- ***Validating business needs***: Marsha decided to use the 5 Whys technique (as referenced in 3.15 Problem Shaping and Reframing) to both validate and develop a shared understanding of the business needs and goals John wanted to achieve. John was instrumental in helping everyone understand how even a small improvement in trading floor efficiencies could result in significant return on investment (ROI) and lead to a competitive advantage for their firm.

By applying the 5 Whys technique iteratively, Marsha was able to determine that the root cause of some of the recent loses stemmed from specific models currently being used for option pricing. It established that there was a clear business need to improve trading decisions through better analytical approach for predicting price movements. Marsha determined that the next step should involve investigating how existing models work.

- ***Validating assumptions***: Marsha approached the Quants team and the Risk team to understand the existing prediction models in depth. The Quants team and Risk team stated that those isolated losses were expected and as part of market risk, simply a cost of doing business. Marsha decided to pursue this further and suggested they test the assumptions associated with the current models. The Quants team outlined that their models are based on two primary assumptions. The Black Scholes model assumes that option prices follow a log-normal distribution and prices can be essentially predicted based on current spot price (current market price) and the historical volatility (standard deviation). The RiskMetrics™ model is an auto-regressive time series model. In simple terms it says yesterday's price has more weight than the price that was the day before. Hence, future prices can be predicted by creating a weighted average model. Similarly, the Risk team stated that the daily limits (VaR) are set by determining the probability of loss at a certain confidence interval (for example, 95%) and it assumes either Black-Scholes model or RiskMetrics in determining underlying distribution. These model characteristics indicate that the assumption around losses are valid and there may be possibilities to better predict these losses using more variety in the data used.
- ***Utilizing business knowledge***: Marsha noted that these model assumptions are based on very limited historical trading data, and other equally important data was being ignored. For example, the effect of the news cycle was not taken into consideration, type of industry of the underlying stock was not considered, and other macro parameters like GDP, interest rate spreads, and underlying asset fundamentals could also be part of the predictive approach. When Marsha outlined these, the operations reps and the traders stated that they always follow foreign markets, daily news, and sometimes Twitter before triggering the trades.
- ***Demonstrating outcome with plausible solutions***: Based on previous experience, Marsha realized that without describing a potentially feasible solution option, it would be easy for attendees to get "bogged down in the details" of today's challenges, or worse yet, jump to one of the technology solutions that John had seen at the conference. She started illustrating the business opportunity in more concrete terms and outlined some recommendations to improve trading floor efficiencies:
  - Marsha described a future vision of a new predictive model for trading floor operations by describing benefits that could be derived.

She focused on key benefits that would appeal to various stakeholders at the workshop:

1. Improve confidence of trades by providing more information to traders (improve the availability of relevant information on trade terminals and presentation of heterogenous data).
2. Limit undue risks to overall book of business (parallel pilot with existing models and/or pilot with arbitrage trades that involve low risk opportunities).
3. Track the performance of the new model (measure the opportunity cost when trades are not executed based on the new model).
4. Retain oversight on trades and risk levels (VaR) to maintain regulatory compliance (explore how risk levels can be employed for the new predictive model).
5. Train traders to utilize the new predictive model results.

Marsha also mentioned that the exercise is not only developing a new predictive model for option trading; it would also impact various other operations. For example, it would include application development (1, 2), process optimization (1, 2, 3, 5), integrating enterprise data sources for big data implementation (1), and business intelligence (4) components. Marsha concluded the workshop on a high note by describing the business opportunity in detail and attendees enthusiastically agreed that developing a plan for executing this work was the required next step.

.4 Key Takeaways

- It can be challenging to achieve the desired future state without ensuring stakeholder alignment and understanding. The starting point is not necessarily implementation of new technology but instead developing a shared understanding of the problem that needs to be addressed.
- Clearly articulating the need and business problem requires a significant amount of upfront analysis. For example, in this scenario, the business problem could lead to five considerations, which could include initiatives beyond analytics. Without considering all aspects of a business problem, an analytics solution may be misaligned to the overall business objective.
- When reviewing existing analytics processes or models, verify the principles on which the model was built. This often leads to discovery of limitations in the existing models and leads to better solutions. For example, by examining the model assumptions such as distribution of option prices being log-normal (Black-Scholes model) or higher weight is given to more recent option prices, while predicting future options prices (RiskMetrics) shows that no other parameters are considered in the analytics model.
- Correctly applying effective business analysis techniques such as a workshop leads to collective problem analysis by different stakeholder groups. Through shared understanding and hearing different perspectives, root causes can be uncovered and problems can be effectively prioritized for solving.

2.2 Source Data

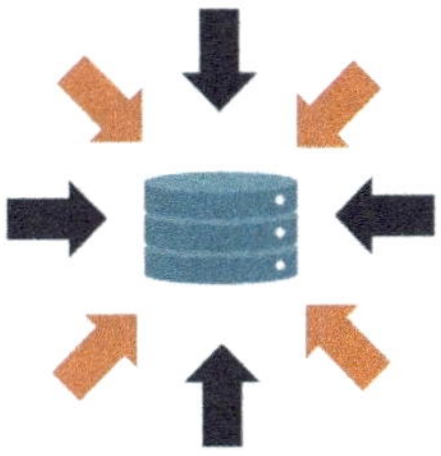

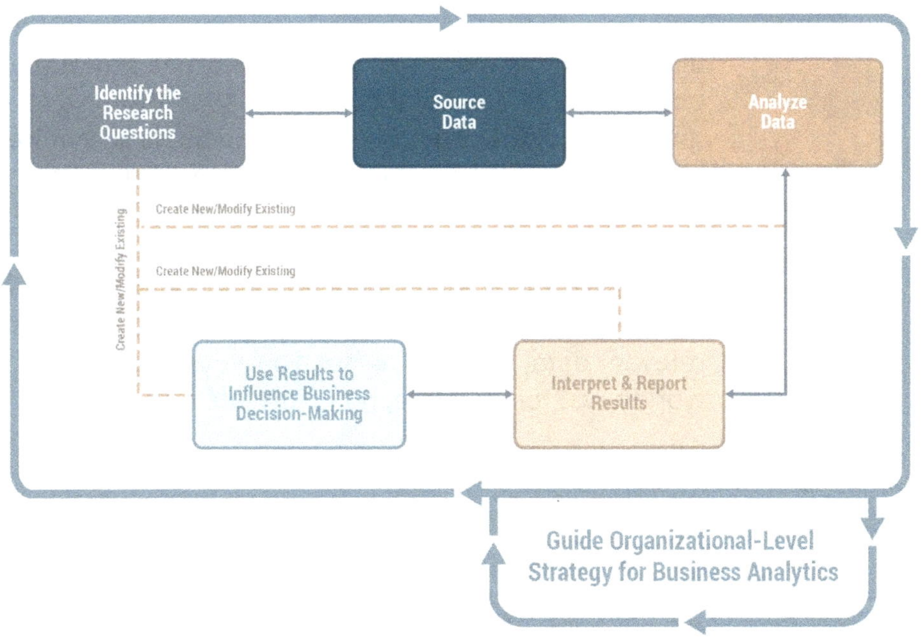

The Source Data domain is a top-down exercise to determine the right data needed for a given research question.

The tasks within the Source Data domain are performed by individuals who possess strong technical skills related to the data architecture of the organization and the skills required to extract or make the relevant data available from different data sources. While these tasks are critical and require the most amount of effort, the starting point of sourcing data is a top-down exercise. The first and foremost exercise in sourcing data is related to understanding the context of the problem and determining what type of data must be used.

In some organizations, this may be the task of a data analyst, data scientist, or a business analysis professional. While data scientists see datasets as a set of variables, it is the business analysis professional who brings the insight to determine whether a dataset might be useful to explore within a business context. Business analysis professionals understand the meaning behind data variables; in essence, the importance of the data to the organization. Because of these differences in viewpoints, a well-structured data analytics team includes professionals who collectively provide both business and data science skills when sourcing data.

Tasks in the Source Data domain include:

- Plan Data Collection,
- Determine the Data Sets,
- Collect Data, and
- Validate Data.

2.2.1 Plan Data Collection

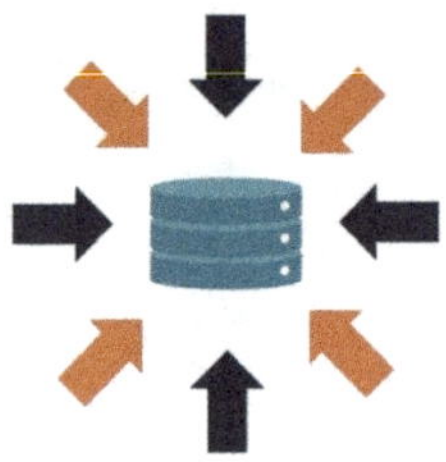

Before data can be sourced, analysis is performed to determine what data is most relevant to the analytics problem. Analysts play a significant role in understanding and suggesting relevant data that may provide the expected outcome for the analytics problem before any significant data sourcing and mining activities can be performed. The data required may be internally available within the organization or may require external sources. In certain cases, active data collection may be required directly from the customers. Some data may not be available due to privacy rules while other data may only be available during specific time frames. It requires choosing a representative group for data collection, designing surveys that will result in relevant data, embedding such surveys into business processes and workflows (for example, point-of-sale surveys).

When planning data collection, analyst consider:

- what data is needed,
- the availability of the data,
- the need for historical data,
- determining when and how the data will be collected, and
- how the data will be validated once collected.

Analysts support the data professionals with data sourcing which involves identifying the data required to answer the research questions. This work includes determining the data that is currently collected (whether used or not) and the data which is currently not collected but would help answer the analytics problem. Data sourcing involves determining which sources to use for that data and includes types of systems that house that data (for example: sales, financial, inventory) or data structures that collate that data (for example: data lake, data mart, data vault, data warehouse). If the data is available from multiple sources, then the task involves determining the best source to use with the right level of granularity. Data sourcing often involves collaboration with the architecture team who can share valuable insights into recommended sources as well as compliance with legal regulations, data privacy, and architecture principles.

Non-functional requirements are also considered when planning data collection. This includes privacy, security, retention, volume, timing, integration, and frequency requirements along with any constraints imposed by data availability and existing service level agreements.

Analysts look for situations where the data may have both short- and long-term effects on business decision-making and determine how this influences the frequency of data collection. When the frequency and timing needs for the business data analytics efforts are greater than what is currently happening, an assessment of costs to obtain the data at a more regular interval occurs.

Consideration is given to the level of effort required to obtain the data. Data sourced internally may be easier and cost less to obtain than data obtained from external sources. How much the data needs to be manipulated once obtained may influence sourcing decisions as well. For example, if there is a choice between obtaining data directly from a centrally managed data warehouse or pulling data from a peripheral secondary source where the data has already been manipulated into a more usable form, an assessment of data quality may be needed to help determine the best source. A direct pull of data and subsequent data manipulation may mean a little more work and overhead cost, but that might be acceptable if the post-massaged data from the secondary source is questionable from a quality perspective. Analysts also determine how much data will be structured versus unstructured and determine how much of each type is feasible to use.

- ***Structured data*** is data that is organized, well-thought-out and formatted, such as data residing in a database management system (DBMS). Structured data is easily accessed by initiating a query in a query language such as SQL (standard query language).
- ***Unstructured data*** is the exact opposite of structured data as it exists outside of any organized repository like a database. Unstructured data takes on many forms and sources such as text from word processing documents, emails, social media sites, image, audio, or video files.

There is significantly more work involved to organize unstructured data for analysis. Consideration is given to if the unstructured data will be useful and how it will be used. While unstructured data might be more complex, the challenges can be minimized depending on whether the team has the necessary tools, experience, and skills.

Once a data collection plan is created, stakeholders who are impacted or possess some ownership over the data review the plan along with the analytics team. Analysts take responsibility for facilitating the team to consensus in order to obtain approval of the data collection approach.

When planning data collection, analysts use various elicitation techniques to acquire the information necessary to build the data collection plan. Brainstorming with the business and technical domain experts provides a quick list of data sources to consider. Document analysis is used to identify data sources through the review of existing architecture models. Skills such as organization and solution knowledge provide context and insights when developing a data collection approach. Problem-solving, identifying data sources, and decision-making are used when facilitating discussions with those who approve the data collection plan.

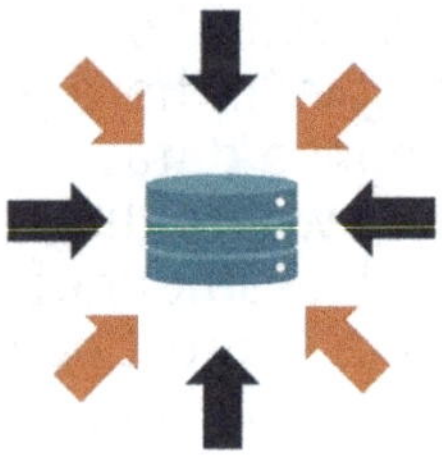

Importance of Industry Knowledge in Sourcing Data

Customer insolvency is one of the big concerns in subscriber-based business models. For instance, in telecom a timely and accurate identification of customers who do not pay their bills can result in significant savings for the companies.

One approach to identifying data for such a scenario can be to look at customer behaviour towards past payments. However, an analyst with sufficient industry knowledge may recommend call detail records (CDR) to be considered as an additional data requirement. CDR consists of call transactions and identifiers of each call that originates from a given mobile number. For example, CDR may assist in determining a trend in call volumes for a particular account. Likewise, analysts may suggest investigating customer profile data to identify new customers. There is a higher percentage of new customers who do not pay than existing customers. Geo-location data gathered from mobile devices and cell tower data can also be considered to understand if a mobile phone is dormant over a period. CDR, customer profile data, geo-location, and cell tower data can be used to strengthen the insights that may not be achieved by simply investigating past payment data.

Identification of the right data that may be useful for a given analytics problem is heavily influenced by the industry knowledge available to the analytics team. An analyst may use multiple techniques such as process analysis, concept modelling, and discovery workshops to uncover the business context to determine the type of data needed.

2.2.2 Determine the Data Sets

Determining data sets involves performing a review of the data expected from the data sources and determining specifics such as data types, data dimensions, sample size, and relationships between different data elements. It involves deciding which whole, and which partial, datasets need to be collected. For example, determining whether to use an entire spreadsheet versus specific rows within it. When the required data is not available, determining data sets also involves identifying data gaps. Data gaps occur when data doesn't exist or is missing due to errors such as a failure in the data collection process.

Analysts collate and assess data by establishing relationships between different data elements and identifying data linkages between data from various sources. They may use data discovery tools or database querying to assess data availability.

A five Vs assessment (volume, velocity, variety, veracity, value) helps to determine which datasets to consider:

- ***Volume***: is determined by the amount of data being produced and the size of the data sets needing to be processed.
- ***Velocity***: is determined by the speed at which data is generated and the frequency by which the data needs to be collected and processed.
- ***Variety***: is determined by the variety of data sources, formats, and types needing to be processed.

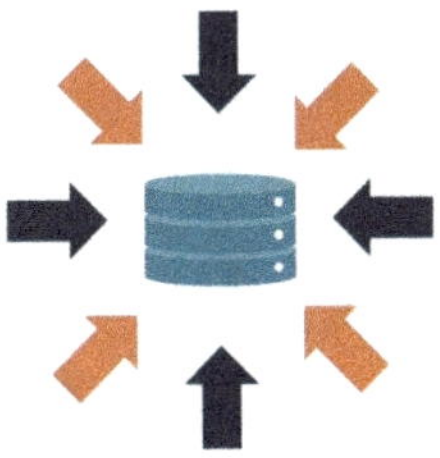

- ***Veracity***: refers to the trustworthiness of the data and that which presents uncertainties and inconsistencies in the data.
- ***Value***: refers to the necessity of driving any analytics exercise from real, valuable business goals.

Non-functional requirements and existing service level agreements may constrain the availability of data. For example, privacy or security considerations may deem a dataset unfit for use.

Analysts possess a firm understanding of the lexicon used by the different business units and are capable of drawing comparisons and relationships between different data sets having the same meaning. Analysts also possess strong visualization skills and contribute to creating conceptual architectural diagrams that depict the data sources, data flows, and frequency of the data feeds. Such models are essential when facilitating discussions about data sourcing with stakeholders and facilitating approvals.

Analysts support data scientists by analyzing the cost versus benefits of different data sets. It is ideal for the analytics team to collect their own data from scratch to reduce any external biases during data collection, but frequently there are not enough resources to do so. Analysts advise on the advantages and disadvantages of using different data sets from a cost, value, timing, risk, and feasibility perspective. This is especially important when the data needed for analytics must be acquired from an external third party. Certain research questions may need to be dropped when it is determined too expensive to obtain the data required to answer it.

When determining data sets, analysts use a variety of techniques to help them work with and understand the data before building their analytical models. Data profiling is used to assess the content, structure, and quality of data. Data sampling is used when breaking a large source of data into a smaller, more manageable set of data. Sampling helps an analyst reduce the amount of data they have to work with as it provides a means to use a representative subset of the larger population. Skills such as creative thinking and conceptual thinking are useful when formulating ideas about which data to use. Business acumen helps the analyst determine which data sets may be best to use based on the current business situation.

2.2.3 Collect Data

Collecting data involves the activities performed to support data professionals with data setup, preparation, and collection. The degree of involvement analysts have with data collection depends on how the organization structures the analytics team as well as the technical abilities of analysts.

In a broad sense, there are two approaches to data collection:

- ***Passive Data Collection***: unobtrusive data collection from users in their day-to-day transactions with the organization. This type of data is available without an analytics objective in mind, and a large portion of such data may already exist with the organization. For example, point-of-sale data, internet browsers, web, and mobile data. This type of data is often curated or transformed to be used for research questions.
- ***Active Data Collection***: actively seeking information from stakeholders for a specific goal. This type of data is not readily available with the organization (surveys and self-reports). Analysts play a significant role in structuring and applying best practices to design the data collection initiative. For example, the analyst may use best practices to design a survey on how to formulate open or closed-ended questions, use of a rating scale like the Likert scale, paired-comparisons, the number of questions, and the flow of questions.

Before data professionals begin collecting large amounts of data, it may be necessary to test the data collection approach by using a small number of observations. If the data collection method is a survey, this task might involve piloting the survey with a small population of participants before performing the survey with the larger population. When collecting data, analysts:

- determine if the data will be originated from different sources,
- identify where the data is going to be collected from (for example, database, spreadsheet, other sources), and
- understand where the data comes from, what transformations are performed, and where it is finally stored in order to assess data quality. This is referred to as data lineage.

When data is collected from different sources, analysts determine if the disparate sources represent the same data in the same way. For example, if data source A uses numeric codes to specify gender and data source B uses alpha codes, the need for reconciling data elements across sources needs to be identified.

The file format for the output produced from each source is also identified. Further analysis determines if the data needs to be formatted prior to merging it into a single file. For example, will spaces need to be removed when moving data from a text file to a spreadsheet? Will data formats need to change so data is consistent between sources? There are instances where data discrepancies cannot be programmatically identified. These require domain knowledge to interpret the same type of data with different labels with the same meaning in different data sources. As data is collected, it is analyzed to identify potential problems with the data collection approach.

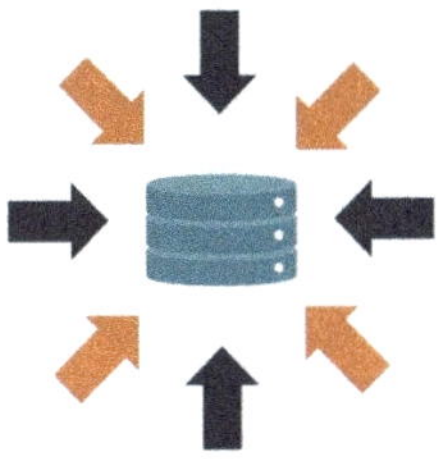

When collecting data, analysts leverage techniques such as surveys and experiments. Data collection is usually performed using automated tools over business processes. Data analysis skills determine what data to use, how to collect it, and its relevance and relationship to what is being analyzed. Demonstrating skills such as trustworthiness and ethics helps to build trust and rapport with stakeholders who may be needed to gain access to data or participate in elicitation activities. Business acumen is necessary during the testing of the data approach and when profiling data.

2.2.4 Validate Data

Validating data involves assessing that the planned data sources can and should be used and, when accessed, the data obtained are providing the types of results expected. Since a detailed analysis of the data is yet to be performed, the objective of validation at this point is high-level.

Business validation involves having the business stakeholders approve the data sources and establish the acceptance criteria that define the parameters for assessing the accuracy of the data. It also includes validating any relevant requirements. For example, if the outcome of data analysis is expected to be a report, business validation involves validating the format and data elements to be included in the report. Technical validation involves technical testing and validation to assess data quality. There are several characteristics reflected in high-quality data, such as:

- ***Accuracy***: the data is correct and represents what was intended by the source. Accurate data is not misleading. Accuracy might be assessed by comparing numbers displayed by a front-end system with data retrieved from the database.
- ***Completeness***: the data is comprehensive and includes what is expected and nothing is missing. Completeness might be assessed by ensuring required fields do not include null values.
- ***Consistency***: how reliable the data is. Data values are consistent when the value of a data element is the same across sources. Consistency might be assessed by ensuring only date values are being displayed in date fields.
- ***Uniqueness***: data that is unique is valuable to an organization. Uniqueness might be assessed by determining whether any duplicates exist in the data.
- ***Timeliness***: data that is fresh and current is more valuable than data that is out of date. Timeliness might be assessed by determining whether the data being received is for the period being requested.

Data validation may be performed by a data analyst, data scientist, or business analysis practitioner with sufficient skills to use the necessary tools to access data and the underlying competencies to analyze the results. Business validation is performed by key stakeholders with the authority to approve data sources for use in analytics initiatives and the knowledge to assess data accuracy in collaboration with the analysts.

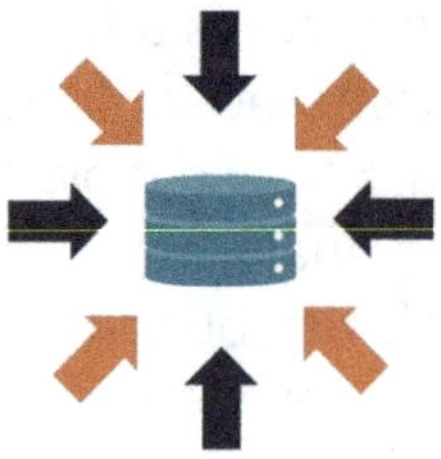

When validating data, analysts use techniques such as data mapping and business rules analysis. Data mapping is used to create a source-to-target data map to define the mapping between the data sources being used and the target system. Business rules analysis provides an understanding of the business rules governing the data by providing guidance as to what should be validated. Conceptual thinking skills help make sense out of the large sets of disparate data sources under analysis and to draw relationships and understanding from the data. Business knowledge provides context to the data being validated, helping analysts determine if the data is accurate and complete.

2.2.5 Select Techniques for Source Data

The following is a selection of some commonly used analysis and analytics techniques applicable to the Source Data domain. The list of techniques presented does not represent a comprehensive set of techniques used by an analyst in the Source Data domain but presents a small, but useful, set of techniques that can be used.

Techniques	Usage Context for Business Data Analytics	***BABOK®* *Guide* v3.0 Reference**
Acceptance and Evaluation Criteria	Used for determining the correct data and to validate data by understanding applicable criteria from both business and technology perspectives so that the right data can be sourced.	Chapter 10.1
Data Dictionary	Used to create a dictionary of terminologies to describe the data labels that can be applied consistently to prepare datasets which can be used throughout the life cycle of an analytics initiative.	Chapter 10.12
Data Flow Diagrams	Used to understand the conceptual or logical view of the data being collected and stored within data sources used for planning and data validation.	Chapter 10.13
Data Modelling	Used to organize data elements and their interrelationships in conceptual, logical, and physical form in order to identify and validate the right data sources.	Chapter 10. 15
Document Analysis	Used to gather information about various internal source systems.	Chapter 10.18
Interface Analysis	Used to understand how data is captured and stored in relevant data sources. Such analysis is useful in cases where an interface may request multiple data elements but stores information differently.	Chapter 10.24
Non-Functional Requirements Analysis	Used for identifying and analyzing quality and governance attributes such as privacy, volume, frequency, retention, integrity, and constraints related to data sources to formulate a data collection plan.	Chapter 10.30

Techniques	Usage Context for Business Data Analytics	*BABOK® Guide* v3.0 Reference
Survey or Questionnaire	Used as a form of actively collecting data which may not be available readily but may be required for the analytics initiative.	Chapter 10.45
Data Mapping	Used to develop traceability between data elements and data sources with the data owner, availability, frequency, constraints, assumptions, transformations, and extraction/ collection methods to build a reference for data collection.	N/A
ETL and Data Management Techniques	Used to collect data without impacting the business continuity of an organization.	N/A

2.2.6 A Case Study for Source Data

Voice termination fraud is a major concern in the telecom industry; billions of dollars are lost by telecom companies according to industry research.

.1 The Challenge

Voice termination fraud, also referred to as SIMbox fraud, often occurs when international calls are hijacked by an intermediate network party and the call traffic is routed via Voice over Internet Protocol (VoIP) and then injected back through SIMboxes that are local to the receiving country. These practices effectively bypass the fees owed to telecom carriers resulting in lost revenue for the telecom industry.

Consider Alice in Country A who is making a phone call to Bob in Country B (a different country), as depicted in the graphic below. Instead of the call moving through the legal least cost path between the two countries, it moves through a SIMbox to a fraudulent least cost path carrier.

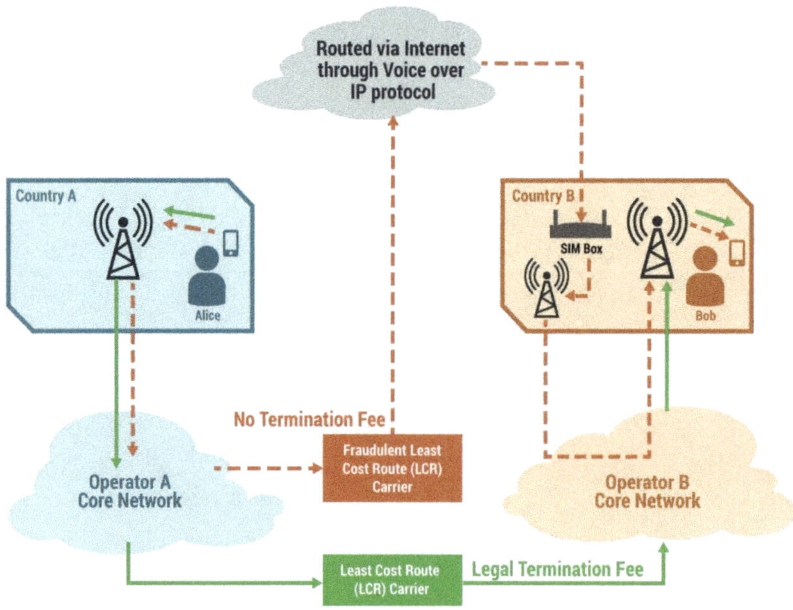

A SIMbox is a legal device, but they can be used by individuals to re-route cell phone calls to VoIP, in order to bypass the receiving network carrier, who would have received a termination fee for providing the last mile connectivity for calls. This reduces the money collected and overall revenues of the telecom as well as voice quality and fidelity of the networks.

Context

Traditional detection methods are inaccurate when detecting SIMbox fraud. SIMbox network signatures are difficult to track and emulate genuine devices like network repeaters or probes. Plus, the volume of device data generated is extremely large in size and variety.

This is especially a problem in Africa and Southeast Asia as the local call rates are cheaper compared to global averages. A Nigerian telecom carrier plans to use recent advancements in predictive analytics to detect and limit voice termination frauds in real-time. Adaku Musa, an experienced telecom expert with the telecom carrier, was asked to assist the data analysis team in her organization to develop a solution that could predict real-time fraudulent traffic in the network.

.2 Identifying Options

As an experienced telecom expert, Adaku was well aware of recent technological advancements. She assessed the situation and recommended three methods to support the objectives of this work:

Analysis Steps	Explanation	Advantages	Disadvantages
Identify SIMbox characteristics	Place test calls to own network from a foreign country through a calling card and identify if the last leg of a call is routed through SIM cards. This can be used to discover rules to identify SIMboxes and apply these rules in data collection and transformation in more sophisticated analysis.	Easy to apply for discovering SIMbox characteristics/rules. For example: • Large volumes of outgoing calls. • Different destinations. • Low number of incoming calls within the network.	• Although SIMboxes can be identified with such an approach it is hard to scale for multiple countries. • It is not real-time detection and rule-based. Identification may not be highly accurate.

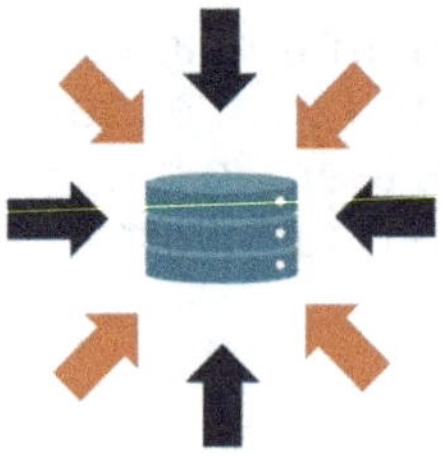

Analysis Steps	Explanation	Advantages	Disadvantages
Passive call detail records (CDR) analysis with data sampling	Analyze CDR to create a baseline for relevant data that may be used for predicting/ classifying a call whether it is genuine or not. The rules discovered in the earlier stage are used to derive the right predictors and formats. For example, CDR may provide individual call duration, but volume of outgoing call for a SIM/ subscriber is an aggregate level data which may be a true predictor.	• Sampling of data from CDR provides a quicker way to test the hypothesis based on the rules above without the need to analyze all the CDR.	• It is not real-time detection of SIMbox fraud; however, it is used to determine the right predictor variables and allows the data science team to quickly train and test classification algorithms that can be deployed in real-time. • Less accurate than a complete analysis of CDR due to sampling errors.
Analysis of CDR utilizing big data technologies	Analyze CDR using different big data technologies to discover additional predictor variables that may affect the classification of fraud. This step could have been performed before sampling in the previous step; however, it would have taken more time, effort, and cost to do so.	• More accurate than analysis using sampling. • No need to analyze already established predictors as the analysis is carried forward from last stage. • Can be implemented in real-time.	• Expensive and requires technical and data sophistication.

.3 Outcomes Achieved

It is important to note that each method builds on the previous analysis in an iterative manner and provides an escalation in approach and successively more accurate information. The data itself goes through several layers of transformation. Business data analytics tools and techniques, as well as strong business knowledge, were used throughout to identify the actual predictors and rules that would be useful for predicting fraud.

The following identifies the results of the analysis and lists the data that was used to determine the appropriate predictors for fraud analysis:

CDR Information Directly Available

Partial CDR Fields (Call Level)	Description
Time	Date and time of the call
Duration	Call duration
Originating Number	Caller's number
Originating Country Code	Caller's country identifier
Terminating Number	Receiver's number
Terminating Country Code	Receiver's country code
IMEI	International mobile equipment ID
IMSI	International mobile subscribers ID
LAC ID	Local area base station identifier

Transformed Information used for Prediction

Transformed Data (SIM Level)	Description
IMSI	International mobile subscriber's ID
Total # Calls/ day	Total number of calls per day
Total numbers called	Total number of unique subscribers called on a single day
Total Night Calls	Total number of night-time calls
Total Incoming	Total number of incoming calls to the subscriber
Average Minutes	Average call duration of each subscriber
Most Frequent LAC ID	Most frequent base station used for calls
Most frequent Originating Country	Most frequent originating country identifier
Most frequent Terminating Country	Most frequent terminating country identifier

In this case, the data identified in the first table was directly available. Using domain knowledge and successive data transformation approaches, the data depicted in the second table was created to support the predictive analytics outcomes. This data improves the predictive power of any SIMbox fraud detection algorithm.

By progressing through this structured approach, analyzing the data, and utilizing appropriate business data analytics techniques, Adaku could determine the best set of predictors that her organization could use to develop the fraud classification algorithm.

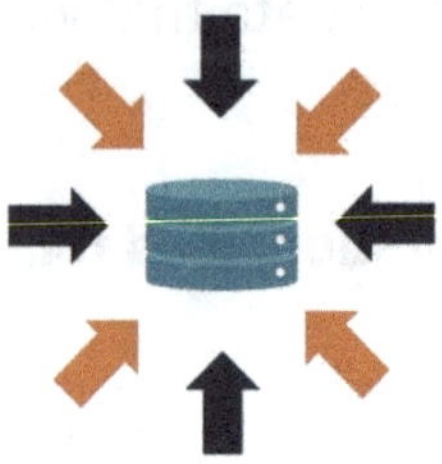

.4 Key Takeaways

- A structured approach to planning data collection and how that data can be used results in more accurate analysis and subsequent prediction of fraud.
- Industry knowledge, business knowledge, and solution knowledge are key competencies to help identify the most relevant data. In this case, Adaku's knowledge of how SIMbox fraud takes place pointed her to the CDR as the right data source.
- The available data may not be directly useful in analysis and undergoes additional transformation to serve its intended use. In this case, the data captured in the CDR was not sufficient in its raw form and application of business knowledge was needed to transform the data to a more business-oriented format for better analytical insights.
- By successive experimentations and analysis of the outcomes, more accurate methods might emerge. In this case, we saw the refinement of data and methods (rule-based discovery to passive CDR analysis to real-time big data implementation) to achieve the desired outcomes.

2.3 Analyze Data

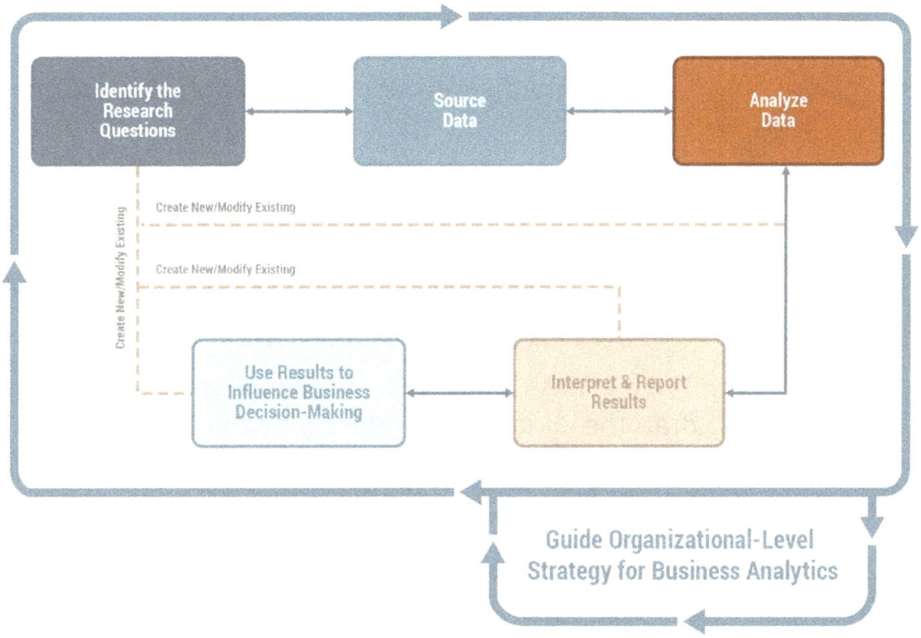

Analyzing data involves deciding how data analysis will be performed, including which models and mathematical or statistical techniques will be used. Analyzing data also involves:

- preparing the data for analysis,
- performing the data analysis,
- determining whether the analytical solution/results are helping to answer the business question, and
- making adjustments to the approach when they do not.

When analyzing data, the business analysis professional is more likely to support the data scientist than to be responsible for running the analytical models themselves. A business analysis professional brings the required domain knowledge for the area under analysis to the team, providing context to the problem or opportunity the analytics effort is aiming to address. The data scientist, requiring a strong understanding of the business considerations, may not possess that knowledge themselves. Strong collaboration between the data scientist and the business analysis professional ensures that the analytics work is performed within the correct business context.

Tasks in the Analyze Data domain include:

- Develop Data Analysis Plan,
- Prepare Data,
- Explore Data,
- Perform Data Analysis, and
- Assess the Analytics and System Approach Taken.

2.3.1 Develop Data Analysis Plan

The data analysis plan may be formal or informal. The objective is to ensure sufficient time to plan the data analysis activities required for the initiative.

When developing the data analysis plan, the analyst determines:

- which mathematical or statistical techniques the data scientist plans to use,
- which statistical and algorithmic models are expected for use (such as regression, logistics regression, decision trees/random forest, support vector machines, and neural nets),
- which data sources will be used and how data will be linked or joined, and
- how data will be preprocessed and cleaned.

The business analysis professional provides insights into the plan or may draft the initial plan for review by the data scientist. It is the data scientist who possesses deep technical expertise to decide how the data analysis will be conducted. Analysis skills are applied by ensuring sufficient information about the business domain is provided to the data scientist so an effective approach to data analysis is developed. Analysts understand the mathematical techniques and algorithmic models in sufficient detail to explain the analysis approach to business stakeholders: why a particular model may be chosen for the given research question.

If the data analysis plan is formally documented, analysts use templates to ensure consistency and guide planning decisions. Analysts use metrics and key performance indicators to assist the data scientist in determining if the outcomes from data analysis are producing the results required to address the business need. Organizational knowledge helps business analysis professionals provide the context for the data scientist's work.

Planning Business Data Analytics Approach at Various Stages

Analysts may not require a rigorous understanding of the various algorithmic models used in predictive analytics exercises, but it is helpful to understand these at a high-level. A foundational understanding of these models help analysts describe what models are being considered, and why, to stakeholders.

A limited sample of different models is presented below with some of their advantages and disadvantages.

Model Name	Description	Advantages	Disadvantages
Ordinary Least Squares Regression	This model uses linear regression. A linear relationship can be established between predictor variables and the independent variable by minimizing the squared errors between observed values and the predictions.	• Used extensively • Easy to understand and explain	• May perform poorly due to simple construct
ARIMA Method (Auto-Regressive Integrated Moving Average)	Primarily used for time-series data analysis. For example, stock movements based on moving averages and data trends.	• Can handle time-series data with trends	• Slowly getting phased out by more accurate algorithms
Decision Trees	Variables are iteratively chosen that can separate the predictions into buckets with the maximum number of observations.	• Easy to understand and visualize • Decision rules can be extracted	• May have generalization errors (may perform poorly if the future data is significantly different from the training data)
Random Forest	Takes many shallow decision trees and combines the result through voting.	• Works in most cases with high accuracy	• Complex to explain the result • Too general a purpose

Model Name	Description	Advantages	Disadvantages
Logistic Regression	Maximizes the probability difference between different classes.	• Used for primarily binary classification	• Can have a high bias towards model assumptions • Requires preprocessing and normalization of data
KNN (K-Nearest Neighbors)	Classifies new data based on its distance to other nearest data points.	• General-purpose algorithm	• Too many modelling assumptions • Fails in higher dimensions
Naïve Bayes (NB)	Based on computing conditional probabilities of data and predicting the outcome.	• Works well with text processing	• There are better algorithms that outperform NB • NB gives conditional independence assumption that will affect the posterior probability estimate
SVM (Support Vector Machine)	Maximizes the margin between two disparate classes of data.	• Good performance for image, video use cases	• Requires specific hyperparameter tuning expertise (algorithms)
Perceptron	Fewer model assumptions and a building block for neural nets and deep learning.	• Easy to understand • Chained together in a neural network (NN) to produce accurate predictions.	• Extremely complicated when used in neural networks • Low performance outside a neural network

2.3.2 Prepare Data

Preparing data involves obtaining access to the planned data sources and establishing the relationships and linkages between sources in order to create a coherent dataset. Data scientists identify how different datasets are related, consider whether the data can be linked in theory, and decide whether it can happen in practice.

Preparing data includes understanding the relationships that exist between data. For example, do two tables have a 0 to 1, 1 to 1, or 1 to many relationships? Preparing data also involves establishing the joins or linkages between sources, normalizing data to reduce data redundancy, standardization, scaling, and converting data. Sometimes the data collected is uninterpretable and must be transformed to lend value to the analytics effort. Data cleansing is a process by which data is transformed to correct or remove bad data.

Data preprocessing, scaling, normalization, imputation, and cleansing are some of the common terminologies used in analytics.

Data scientists identify the rules for consolidating data, perform the consolidation, and then validate the results to see if the business rules are being adhered to. Any mechanisms data scientists build to automate the data acquisition or preparation processes can be repurposed for use by other analytics teams.

Data scientists leverage a host of techniques when preparing data. Weighting is one technique applied to data to correct bias. Sample weights can be applied to address the probability of unequal samples and survey weights applied to address bias in surveys. Data scientists use strong technical skills and knowledge of statistics when preparing data for use in an analytics initiative.

When preparing data, analysts provide the business context for data that may or may not differ from the statistical interpretation. For example, if there are missing data elements, a data scientist may choose to attribute those elements with mean or median value to retain the distribution of a variable intact. While this may be a sound approach from a statistical point of view, it may conflict with some business rules which the analyst may be able to highlight.

Similarly, if there is a portion of the data with missing information, a data scientist may choose to ignore the observations and continue the analysis because it may be statistically insignificant. But from a business standpoint further investigation may be required to determine the course of analysis. These scenarios are best handled by analysts with facilitation, collaboration, and elicitation skills who can supplement the information by stakeholder collaboration and investigation of the recording process.

2.3.3 Explore Data

Exploring data involves performing an initial exploratory analysis to ensure the data being collected is what was expected from the data sources. It provides a form of quality check to ensure the right type and quality of data is being obtained prior to executing more detailed data analysis work.

Data exploration is primarily the responsibility of the data scientist, but the work is most effectively performed when paired with an understanding of the business domain, an area where a business analysis professional can lend much assistance.

Exploratory analysis involves obtaining a subset of data and identifying initial trends and relationships to develop a fair understanding of the value the data is providing. The data scientist looks for data gaps or data redundancy that signal the data may need to be cleansed, or data outliers (noise) that signal data may need to be excluded. Missing data from a survey could mean a person is missing from the dataset or that a person might have only answered certain questions on a survey. The data scientist assesses the data quality to determine the course of action using the following checkpoints:

- ***Data integrity***: Can the data be trusted? For example, is the data structurally correct?
- ***Data validity***: Is the data truly representative of an underlying construct? For example, is Win ratio a good measure of monthly sales performance?
- ***Data reliability***: If data is collected more than once, will the same results be obtained? For example, will a survey respondent answer a question differently on different days of the week?
- ***Data bias***: Does the data portray an accurate picture of a given situation? It indicates underlying quality issues which may involve issues with integrity, validity or reliability. For example, are employees over-estimating the quality of their work or do we have a situation where the survey participants are not a representative sample of the population?

Exploratory data analysis is a deeper validation of the quality of data which provides initial insights regarding data behavior or patterns that can be assessed for suitability of the data.

Where possible, and when required, data scientists transform data, removing unrecognized data elements or converting data to a consistent data format when disparate data formats exist. If the data collection processes are not providing a sufficient amount of good data, the data scientist determines a new approach to sourcing the data. This may involve establishing new joins or relationships between data or identifying completely new data sources. It might be necessary to go back and consider whether there are other datasets that could be collected if the first dataset is not usable.

Exploratory data analysis activities are more involved than data preparation activities. They provide opportunities for analysts and data scientists to discover latent data gaps, interrelationships between variables, and allow multiple statistical tests to determine whether data is equitable for the research problem. Once there is an assurance that the data sources are providing the right data, what is learned from the exploratory analysis can be used to guide the approach taken to perform the detailed data analysis.

When exploring data, analysts use data mining to identify information or patterns that require further investigation. Data scientists use a host of data discovery and profiling tools to mine data. They use statistical parameters and visualizations to determine data quality. For example, histograms can be used to understand the distribution of values across variables. Feedback loops are used to allow for adjustments to be made about what techniques and models best fit the data. Ongoing collaboration between the data scientist and the business analysis practitioner pairs the industry and business domain knowledge possessed by the business analyst practitioner with the analysis results produced by the data scientist to determine whether the results are helping to answer the business question.

An Example of Exploratory Data Analysis and its Benefits

Exploratory data analysis is a systematic and iterative approach used for:

- assessing the quality of data,
- providing early insights,
- recognizing derived predictors,
- treating missing data, and
- providing an indication of initial algorithmic models.

An example of the use of exploratory data analysis can seen in the analysis of real estate, where the analytics objective was to predict the value of a property in and around the Boston area. This dataset originates from the University of California, Irvine Machine Learning Repository (https://archive.ics.uci.edu/ml/index.php). Although this data is collected in early 1980's, it can be used to demonstrate the benefits of exploratory data analysis.The data contains 13 predictor variables, including per capita crime rate, the average number of rooms per house, distance to employment centres, commercial property acres per town, age of the property, and so forth. The price of the houses, which is the target variable we are trying to predict, is captured as the median value of the houses in units of $1,000.

When the data was explored, some of the observations for house prices were found to be outliers when compared to most house prices. Although the data exists, it may influence the final predictions hence the data scientist would have to determine whether to exclude the data or not. An analyst can help in this situation by assessing the data collection method to identify if there are any missed business rules. It was found these observations are artificially set to a high value of $50,000 to signify observations where the prices cannot be disclosed. This analysis supports the data scientists remark that some values are outliers and should be excluded from future analysis. The outliers can be graphically seen below around the $50,000 mark.

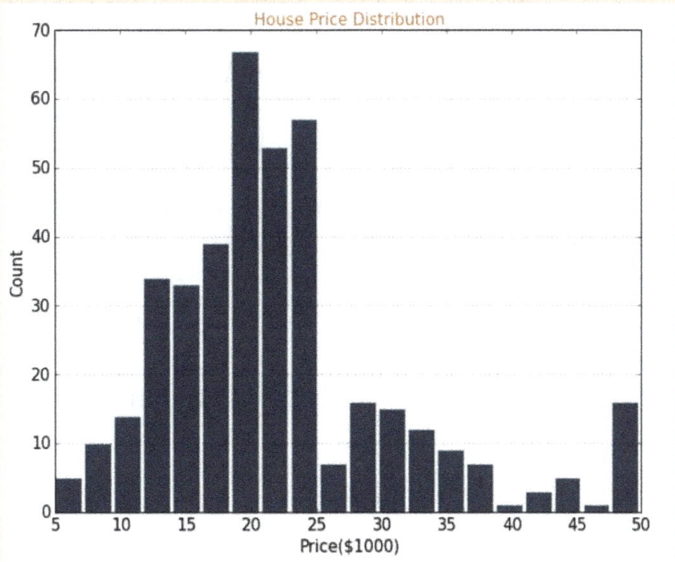

Likewise, when some of the variables are compared against the prices, it was observed that most predictors have a linear relationship with price. For example, some change in the predictor variable changes the price by a proportional amount and has a straight-line relationship, as illustrated below.

(RM - Average rooms per dwelling)

This indicates that a linear model such as Ordinary least squares regression can be used for predicting house prices as a candidate prediction model. In summary, analyst and data scientists can use the outcome of exploratory data analysis to make critical decisions with respect to data quality and modelling approach. The analysts can also use the visuals from the data exploration phase to explain and justify a course of action taken in an analytics exercise.

2.3.4 Perform Data Analysis

Data analysis involves the extensive deep analysis performed once the data quality issues are resolved through exploratory analysis. Performing data analysis involves the application of mathematics, statistics, and the completion of extensive mathematical analyses related to answering the research questions for different stakeholders.

Where exploratory analysis tested the dataset, performing data analysis involves using the results of an exploratory analysis to determine the best mathematical methods and approaches to use and then conducting the in-depth data analysis required to answer the analytics problem. The original research question in the business language is transformed into a mathematical question, which is translated into a model to perform a deeper analysis.

When performing data analysis, data scientists use technical techniques requiring extensive mathematical skills. Some techniques are leveraged to find associations or to cluster data, which is helpful when identifying patterns (for example, association rule learning, decision tree analysis, and K-means clustering.) Many techniques, such as the use of machine learning and artificial intelligence, advance the data scientist's analysis capabilities. Data scientists may use regression analysis to predict and forecast. Simulation can be used to play out a series of actions or behaviours.

Many of the algorithmic models are automated through available machine learning packages, but the parameters and measures of success require significant business domain knowledge to be aligned to the research questions. For example, an organization seeking to discover market segments based on the order history and customer profile data may require some marketing guidance on how the segments should be discovered. It may depend on demography, monetary value, type of products the customers purchase, customer lifetime value, and other factors. The choice of the clustering model may be influenced based on the business direction. Similarly, most of the success criteria for models are also influenced by business decisions that need to be translated into mathematical parameters where analysts may contribute significantly by describing the success criteria to the data scientists.

Data scientists use creative thinking skills to determine different approaches for answering the research question, especially when the data results are not helping to achieve the stated objectives. As with exploratory analysis, the data scientist uses industry and business domain knowledge, and when not present, these skills can be augmented by leveraging the skills of the business analysis professional.

2.3.5 Assess the Analytics and System Approach Taken

Assessing the analytics and system approach taken involves collaborating as an analytics team to determine whether the results from data exploration or data analysis are helping to answer the business question. Assessing the analytics approach is performed iteratively with Explore Data and Analyze Data.

When issues arise with data sourcing or with the results of data analysis, the approach to analytics adapts. For example, when data exploration uncovers issues with data quality or determines the wrong data is being collected, or data gaps are an issue, there may be a need for adjustments to be made to how and where the data is being collected. If the results of data exploration are acceptable, it is still possible the results from data analysis will fail to answer the questions being asked. The results from data analysis may not produce results that help meet the objectives of the initiative.

In these scenarios, data exploration and data analysis tasks are repeated. Iteration occurs between the data exploration and data analysis tasks until the data scientist is comfortable with the data sources being used. Their assessment is based on the quality of data being obtained and its value toward answering the research questions.

When assessing the analytics and system approach taken, business analysis professionals require basic skills in statistics and a basic understanding of data science tools and technologies. They should possess sufficient business acumen to provide context to the data analysis. Business analysis professionals answer questions the data scientist may pose related to the business. Adaptability is necessary to adjust the analysis approach as more data is uncovered, new insights learned, or different levels of stakeholders are involved. Trustworthiness is important as in some industries, having access to certain types of data comes with a great deal of responsibility, often with legal implications. It is important to know what acceptable data use is and what it is not, and what can be accessed or viewed and what cannot.

Real-World Example of Analytics Challenges and Course Correction

In highly competitive markets, organizations struggle to get the right message to the customers, at the right time. To achieve this, marketing teams use "hyper-personalization" to target their messaging to their customers. Whether a particular campaign will have a significant impact on sales is a question of concern for most marketing teams. This is a research problem. For example, what is the likely outcome if a campaign is launched and which potential customers are likely to purchase. This is an example of a question suited for prescriptive analytics.

Consider an organization launching a campaign to offer a 10% discount on a digital product. The organization also wants to reduce the cost of campaigning by limiting the number of customers they want to target.

The organization collected data on 50,000 customers and leads from their CRM system (often referred to as population or population set), and were trying to decide what the campaign will be, in terms of potential customers who will buy the product. The data included variables such as age, geography, gender, different product features, existing customer or not, and has the customer purchased the product in the past or not.

The analytical approach, broadly, was as follows:

- People who have already purchased the product carry certain attributes and people who have similar attributes will likely purchase the product, given a discount.
- Out of the 50,000 customer records, a subset of 30,000 customer records was chosen to train the model (for example, in simple terms, training means to deduce the mathematical construct that predicts the outcome using a subset of data). This training data of 30,000 records included customers who had already purchased the product and some who have not.
- Remaining data within the population set can be used for testing the prediction accuracy by comparing the prediction from the mathematical model versus the testing data (for example, the remaining data) where we know whether the customer has purchased the product or not.

If the test data accuracy is high, the model can be applied to successively larger or different sets of data segments to predict who are likely to purchase the product and the campaign can be exposed to those customers only.

An algorithmic model (for example, logistic regression) was considered and although the training performance was considerably high, the testing performance was found to be low. The data scientist suggested there is a possibility the variable considered may not be a true predictor for the given problem. For example, there are two groups, existing customers and leads, who will have different purchasing behaviour even though the values of the other variables are similar. Additionally, there may be other variables missing from analysis such as income or level of education, which are influencing one or more variables that are part of the analysis and the missing variables may be the true predictors. In statistical terms, these are called confounding variables.

The analytics initiative now has a choice:

- Obtain more relevant data (for example, income and education) with the additional cost of surveys as data may not be available readily.
- Conduct randomized simulation or A/B testing by pursuing purely random customers to study the effectiveness of the campaign but with a higher cost of designing a new experiment and analytical approach.
- Change the analytical approach and models that are better suited where confounding variables are involved such as propensity score matching or random forest methods.

For all these scenarios, the analyst plays a significant role in evaluating and assessing cost-benefit, feasibility, and business impact. This deliberation requires multiple stakeholder discussions and consensus. These are typical business analysis skills in addition to a functional knowledge of analytical methods and concepts.

2.3.6 Select Techniques for Analyze Data

The following is a selection of some commonly used analysis and analytics techniques applicable to the Analyze Data domain. The following list of techniques does not represent a comprehensive set of techniques used by an analyst in the Analyze Data domain but presents a small, but useful, set of techniques that can be used.

Techniques	Usage Context for Business Data Analytics	*BABOK® Guide* v3.0 Reference
Business Case	Used to understand the high-level needs of the business and align the analytics effort to qualify the desired outcome.	Chapter 10.7
Decision Analysis	Used to understand the multiple decision threads and the rationale behind following a particular course of action. For example, the decisions taken by data scientists for data sampling, data transformation, choice of model, and evaluation criteria are validated against the business and statistical parameters.	Chapter 10.16
Financial Analysis	Used to support the decision process by understanding the costs, benefits, financial impact, and business value.	Chapter 10.20
Key Performance Indicators (KPIs)	Used to evaluate the relevant metrics, KPIs, and model criteria to establish the most accurate representation of evaluation parameters for the analytics model. For example, while determining the objective/cost function of a predictive analytics model, KPIs and metrics need to be translated to the mathematical model correctly.	Chapter 10.28
Observation	Used to understand and analyze the data activities and processes to uncover any information that may impact the success of the analytics initiative.	Chapter 10.31
Reviews	Used to understand the whole process of data analytics versus simply evaluating the outcome of the analytics initiative.	Chapter 10.37
Risk Analysis and Management	Used to record and control the inherent risks and assumptions originating due to a certain approach taken for the analytics initiative.	Chapter 10.38
Scope Modelling	Used when re-scoping is needed during the initiative when the analytics objectives, the data, choice of models, or evaluation criteria change.	Chapter 10.41
Data Journalism and Storytelling	Used to communicate the actions and the results of the data analytics initiative to stakeholders in the Analyze Data domain.	N/A

Techniques	**Usage Context for Business Data Analytics**	***BABOK® Guide* v3.0 Reference**
Descriptive and Inferential Statistics	Used to understand the underlying data patterns and signals during exploratory data analysis and modelling. Descriptive statistics is primarily used to describe the data in a more cohesive manner. Inferential statistics is used for predictive and prescriptive modelling (for example, a bayesian inference model).	N/A
Technical Visualizations	Used to understand the underlying patterns and signals from data in a visual format during exploratory data analysis and data modelling. Technical visualizations are used to analyze the data, while business visualizations are used to interpret and report results.	N/A
Machine Learning (ML)/ Deep Learning (DL)	Used to predict or prescribe outcomes. Data scientists understand the mathematical constructs used in ML and DL to achieve a better model performance. Analysts understand and communicate the characteristics of different models. For example, a Naïve Bayes model can be used effectively as spam detection with a cheaper cost of implementation and less data volume.	N/A
Optimization	Used to derive the best possible business outcome where a number of constraints exist. Analysts identify constraints and assess whether it is considered during data analysis and modelling, For example, linear programming in a simple production decision to complex gradient methods for weight optimization in deep learning problems.	N/A
Simulation	Used to derive and demonstrate possible business outcomes when there is a lack of observed data, a high degree of uncertainty, or an extremely high number of modelling parameters are present. Simulation can be effective where the problems may not be solved adequately given the time, schedule, cost, or computing constraints. Even with deep learning and big data technologies, it is sometimes difficult to accurately determine solutions analytically. In such cases simulation is used to solve a problem heuristically. Prescriptive analytics and specifically reinforcement learning problems heavily utilize simulations, for example, monte carlo simulations can be used to generate "good enough" models for estimating a portfolio risk in investment banking and risk management.	N/A

2.3.7 A Case Study for Analyze Data

ABC insurance Co., one of the largest issuers of life insurance in Japan, formed a new data science team comprised of data scientists, actuaries, insurance underwriters, and business data analytics professionals. Their mandate is to challenge the status quo and address existing customer experience challenges. This team promotes new ways of working, including evidence-based decision-making, in the hopes of helping ABC become more responsive to market demands and organizational priorities. In many ways, the goal is to introduce a "start-up culture" into a one-hundred years-old traditionally structured insurance company.

.1 The Challenge

The team conducted a thorough current state analysis of the existing processes that shape customer experience and how ABC uses technology to support its underwriting, quoting, and policy issuing functions. The team identified a number of challenges:

- the application process is cumbersome, taking approximately a month to approve.
- applicants are asked to provide extensive information including demographic information, medical history, and employment information taking 90 minutes to enter.
- they are asked to select among several insurance products or combinations of products

The result? Customers are disengaging, as demonstrated by ABC Insurance's web analytics, which indicate 35% of individuals end their transaction prematurely during the application process.

The team's senior business data analytics expert, Haru Kobayashi, was asked to analyze the data and recommend actions. In addition to reviewing the data collected through the current state analysis, he also analyzed the results of interviews conducted by the team. They interviewed both customers and individuals that abandoned their online applications. Haru analyzed all this data and concluded that consumers are accustomed to seamless online transactions. Respondents acknowledged the need for providing a large amount of information, but they expect the organizations they interact with to provide seamless transactions or risk losing them as a customer.

.2 The Way Forward

The team concluded that ABC's processes are antiquated and inefficient. They believed it was important to make it easier for applicants to submit their information and reduce the time it takes to issue a quote. They also identified the disconnect between an applicant entering information online and the manual processing that takes place to verify information, assess the risk, generate a quote, and respond to the applicant.

The team recommended ABC utilize a technology-based solution, one that delivers a predictive data analytics model and can be customized to accurately classify risk using ABC's standard approach. Using this type of technology can significantly reduce the time taken for approval. The team's immediate goal was to better understand the predictive power of the data from existing underwriting assessments and to enable ABC to use that information to improve the overall process.

.3 Working with Available Data

The team worked with approximately 80,000 customer applications and almost 130 predictor variables. Haru parsed through the data to understand what could be useful and how the data could be used. His initial analysis allowed the team to rationalize data items, understand reasons for missing data, determine what data needs to be input, develop rationale to be followed, and develop a more robust data set.

After transforming the available data, it was categorized into different business relevant data elements such as product information, age, height, weight, employment information, insured information, insurance history, family history, and medical history.

.4 Identifying Key Questions

Initial analysis of the business context suggested that most of the time was spent in risk classification. The team agreed that the biggest reduction in processing time would result from automatically and accurately classifying customer applications to appropriate risk classes. By doing so, the application processing time could be dramatically reduced. Data scientists on the team considered multiple algorithms to produce the desired results. They had some fundamental questions to better understand the data required by underwriters, including:

- How are risk classes related? Do risk classes depend on each other? Are they categorical in nature?
- Is the risk function monotonic?
- Is this a multinomial classification problem?
- What is the best metric to evaluate performance of the predictive model - Accuracy, MCC, or Cohen Kappa?

This terminology and level of expertise may be second nature for data scientists, but business people struggled to understand and the business data analytics professional can play a critical role in helping them understand.

.5 Business Data Analytics Approach

Often, the underlying concepts and mathematical background required to understand data-related challenges turn out to be quite complex. The heavy use of data science terminology by data scientists was not understood by business stakeholders, in this case the underwriters on the team. Likewise, the data scientists were struggling to understand business needs. Haru developed the following approach:

1. Collaborate closely with data scientists to learn terminology.
2. Understand the relevance of the questions asked by the data scientists.
3. Translate this learning to business terms that would be meaningful to underwriters.
4. Communicate the correct business implications so the team could develop a shared understanding of the proposed model.

.6 Outcomes Achieved

Haru worked hard to socialize understanding of several key terms and business rules and helped others understand the impact of their decisions, including:

Key Terms	Application to Predictive Models/ Algorithms
Categorical Risk Classes Insurance risk classes describe groups of individuals with similar risk characteristics. For example, 20-40 years of age, new driver, or smoker may be grouped and classified into a higher risk class and therefore a higher cost to insure.	With this understanding, the team identified categories and determined an effective algorithm to use in the predictive model with output aligned to a single specific risk class (for example, 1 to 8).
Monotonic Risk Function The risk classes are ordinal if the outcome (risk class) follows a specific order. In other words, does risk class 3 have a higher risk profile than risk classes 2 and 1? Similarly, does the risk increase or decrease based on an increasing or decreasing input? For example, the output (likelihood of death) may be monotonic if the input is age.	The behaviour of expected output determines the modelling process. In this case, if an algorithm outputs the probability of the event, then the business stakeholders may have to qualify what the risk classes mean. For example, probability of death of 1-50% may correspond to risk class 1, 50-60% may correspond to risk class 2 and so forth. The modelling must take these aspects into account and that requires a shared understanding between business stakeholders and the team.

Key Terms	Application to Predictive Models/ Algorithms
Multinomial Classification Simply stated, it means that the output of the predictive model is one of the eight risk classes.	Like other classification problems, different parameters such as accuracy, precision, and others can be used, but these parameters may not be robust in evaluating the performance of the predictive model.
Accuracy, Matthews Correlation Coefficient (MCC), or Cohen's Kappa Coefficient These measure algorithm performance. The mathematical background for these metrics needs to be applied for the business context. For example, Cohen's Kappa may be explained in simple terms to the business stakeholder as two underwriters (A and B) are trying to classify the same set of applications independently into two risk classes (for example, 1, 2). Accuracy is the metric that describes the probability or percentage of times both underwriters agree on the risk class for an application. However, underwriters may agree on the risk class by pure chance, say due to lack of information or uncertainty. The Kappa corrects this issue.	The entire focus of modelling and optimization of an algorithm depends upon the definition of success for the algorithm, so it is important to accurately communicate modelling assumptions. The evaluation criteria adopted by the team needs to be communicated to the business stakeholders or there may be other criteria that business stakeholders may think are more relevant (for example, the actuaries may suggest a different one). The success of the entire initiative depends upon what is chosen as the evaluation parameter. Any measure of success must be consistent with the business problem and help create a shared understanding of their use.

Haru's data analysis experience and his ability to bridge the two worlds of data science and business ensured the team achieved its desired outcome.

.7 Key Takeaways

- When data is analyzed from an algorithmic or modelling perspective, the challenge is to translate many of the technically challenging questions to more accessible format for business stakeholders.
- Business data analytics experts combine their business analysis skills with their data analytics skills and leverage underlying competencies such as learning, systems thinking, business acumen, and teaching throughout their work.
- Business data analytics experts play a key role in helping develop shared understanding, including the ability to translate complex data analytics concepts and describe their potential impact on business results. A shared understanding between different teams often forms the first step towards managing the change implications from an analytics initiative.

2.4 Interpret and Report Results

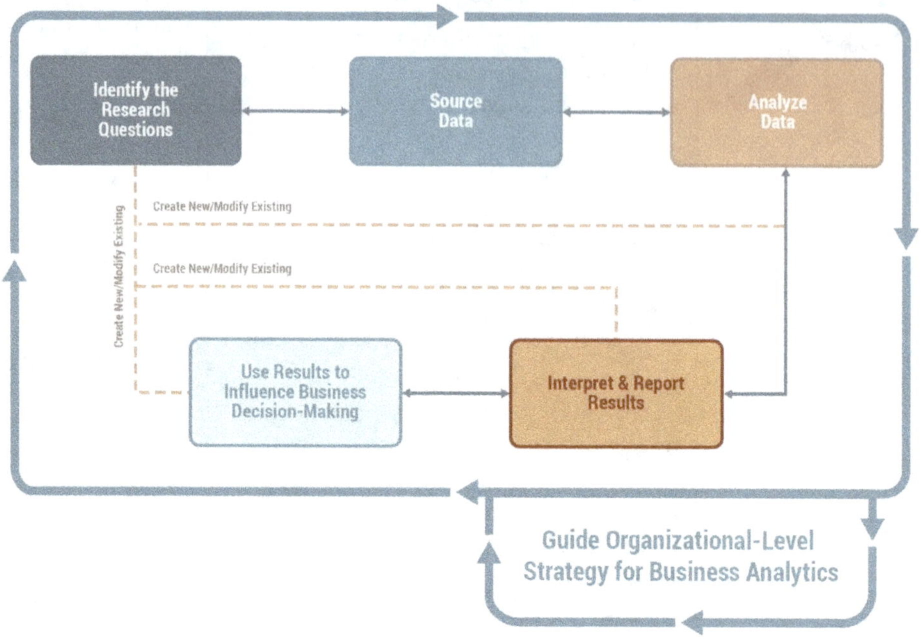

The Interpret and Report Results domain uses the results obtained from data analysis to gain business insights from the data collected and determine how to best communicate and report the outcome from business data analytics to relevant stakeholders.

The term reporting results is used in a broad sense to communicate and explain certain facts to an identified audience.

The outputs from Interpret and Report Results are used to influence decision-making. Business insights may differ from the way data patterns are understood and communicated. Where the data patterns and signals focus on trends, distributions, and statistical parameters, business insights are focused on inferring business-relevant facts. To communicate the insights effectively to the stakeholders, analysts use explanatory analysis rather than exploratory analysis.

The Interpret and Report Results domain includes:

- ***Planning for Communicating the Insights***: Who are the stakeholders that require communication of the insights? What are stakeholder perceptions about the subject matter? What is their level of engagement and availability? What is the desired frequency of communication?
- ***Interpreting Analytics Results***: How are data patterns, trends, signals, and models translated to business insights in business language?
- ***Explaining the Findings***: What is the insight that needs to be communicated? What is the best method of communication? What is the right level of detail for each stakeholder? What is the best way to record the results and feedback for future consumption?

Analysts think like a designer and build the data story with the right visuals to explain the insights that effectively aids decision-making.

Tasks in the Interpret and Report Results domain include:

- Validate Understanding of Stakeholders,
- Plan Stakeholder Communication,
- Determine Communication Needs of Stakeholders,
- Derive Insights from Data, and
- Document and Communicate Findings from Completed Analysis, and
- Select Techniques for Interpret and Reporting Results.

2.4.1 Validate Understanding of Stakeholders

Early in a business data analytics engagement, stakeholders are identified and analyzed to understand how to effectively engage and collaborate with the variety of stakeholders involved. As the engagement evolves, changes to business context, strategy, and personnel occur. As a result, stakeholder analysis is ongoing and continually updated.

The analytics team continually validates the results of stakeholder analysis to help guide their work of interpreting and reporting results. They continually assess:

- changing needs and objectives,
- the importance of the research questions,
- how quickly the analytics results are expected,
- skill-sets for interpreting those results, and
- levels of education in and experience with analytics.

Understanding the unique characteristics of each stakeholder group increases the team's ability to interpret and report meaningful outcomes.

When validating the results of stakeholder analysis, the team uses techniques such as brainstorming, interviews, process modelling, and reviewing other models such as organizational charts. Models that were used to relate the enterprise strategic goals to the organizational goals and objectives and the stakeholders impacted are reviewed. This gives the team the best opportunity to interpret and report results in a way that will resonate with stakeholders.

2.4.2 Plan Stakeholder Communication

Planning stakeholder communication includes identifying what needs to be communicated, to whom it needs to be communicated, how it needs to be communicated, and when it needs to be communicated. Planning stakeholder communication for an analytics initiative is like most other initiative-level communication planning. It requires analysts to know and understand who the stakeholders are and the communication preferences of individual stakeholders and stakeholder groups.

When planning stakeholder communication, analysts consider:

- that stakeholder communications can involve an intermediate or final result since analytics initiatives are inherently iterative.
- the formality and the level of detail may vary amongst stakeholders.
- the level of expertise required by stakeholders to interpret analytics results
- the level of privacy and confidentiality to be maintained.
- keeping stakeholders informed about the progress and the approaches taken throughout the course of the initiative.
- maintaining an appropriate level of communication during the initiative.
- recording the responses and feedback from stakeholders for further action and follow-up.

2.4.3 Determine Communication Needs of Stakeholders

Determining the communication needs of stakeholders enables customization of communications to individual stakeholders or stakeholder groups so the message is clearly understood.

Understanding the characteristics of stakeholders, an output from stakeholder analysis, provides guidance when planning and determining a communication approach. Stakeholder communication requirements may include stakeholder preferences regarding:

- what information is most relevant to them,
- how they wish to receive information,
- how often they wish to be updated,
- who the decision-makers in the stakeholder groups are,
- what biases they carry, and
- what factors can potentially weaken the analysis (such as contradictory results, analytics approach, data anomalies, stakeholders' impact and influence).

Analytics engagements require robust communication as the outcomes and results often point to a gap or a change in business processes that generate friction.

Each stage of the analytics process is communicated in a variety of ways, particularly with regards to the analytics research and experiments that can be quite formal and academic. For example, drug discovery and medical studies impose regulatory formats and structure. Analysts use their understanding of stakeholders to determine how best to communicate. Descriptive and diagnostic analytics results may generate friction when gaps are identified in the business process between stakeholders. Likewise, predictive and prescriptive analytics may suggest a completely new way of decision-making, prompting stakeholders to resist the changes. Analysts find approaches to make the analytics more accessible through compelling ways of representing analytics results.

When planning stakeholder communication, analysts use a variety of elicitation techniques to identify the communication needs of stakeholders and to define the best approach to share the results from analytics. Retrospectives or lessons learned identify what methods of communication worked well and what methods could be improved upon. Facilitation and communication skills, along with business acumen, enable the development of a well thought out communication approach.

2.4.4 Derive Insights from Data

Data scientists and analysts use various methods to understand and derive insights from data. Within the Analyzing Data domain, the first level of inference is drawn from data using various statistical tools, technical visualizations, or data models to understand the patterns. Whether such indications from data are of business relevance and lead to true business insights is determined with appropriate analysis in the Interpret and Report Results domain. For example, there are some surprising insights that were discovered by combining structured and unstructured data when the density of Uber rides was merged with the crime rate for the city of San Francisco. It was observed that the highest number of Uber rides originated from high crime neighbourhoods. Although it is a fascinating correlation, demand prediction for Uber rides should not be modelled on the crime rate without stronger evidence of a relationship. Analysts use a mix of sound statistical judgment and explanatory analysis to translate data patterns to useful insights, especially when the findings are counter to common business practices.

Analysts use multiple visualizations to derive insights from the data collected. Visual models are developed with a variety of data visualization tools. Visualization from a technical perspective differ from visualizations that are intended for business stakeholders. For example, an error residue graph, a technical visualization which shows a decrease in prediction error as the number of predictors increases for a revenue forecasting problem, may be useful for determining the optimum number of variables to use for revenue forecasting. A marketing stakeholder will likely be more interested in a visualization that shows how ad spends relate to overall revenue.

To effectively understand the insight, analysts adopt a design thinking perspective to the visualization and data story explaining the visualization. Inputs from 2.4.3. Determine Communication Needs of Stakeholders play a key role in thinking through the type of visuals or other methods used to clearly articulate the insight and make it business relevant. Both standard (bar graphs and line graphs) and custom visualizations are used to assure meaningful, usable analytics for the business are communicated.

Organizational skills, systems thinking, design thinking, creativity, attention to detail, stakeholder orientation, and industry knowledge are all important skills required to process information and review and assemble the results in an organized fashion. Analysts also require the ability to view results from a holistic viewpoint.

Visualization Best Practices

The ability to effectively derive and explain insights largely depends on visual communication. There is no one size fits all approach to visualization. Forms, graphs, dashboards, and reports are all useful for explaining business insights.

When developing effective visual communications, analysts keep the following practices in mind:

- When there is only a single or a couple of metrics involved, simple text may be a more effective way to communicate the metrics. For example, ROI, profits, percentage, and average values.
- Text, strategically placed to highlight important facts, is a great way to focus attention. Communicate individual insights through their own individual graph increases clarity.
- When there is a limited set of metrics, a tabular summary can be more effective than a graph. The simplest forms of graphs and charts highlight the focal message. Complicated graphs, which are used for visual appeal only, may end up complicating the message. For example, a pie-chart where the audience needs to interpret arc lengths and angles can be replaced with a simple horizontal bar chart.
- 2-dimensional graphs with appropriate colours and labelling can be more effective than 3-dimensional graphs as it is difficult to visualize depth.
- Superimposing graphs with a secondary axis is generally not a good idea. For example, a vertical bar graph showing quarterly revenue and a line graph showing a trend for profit in a single graph with a secondary y-axis will lead to confusion.
- Depending on the context, an interactive or a static graph may be more suitable.
- Statistical or mathematical parameters used in a visual should be explained.

Maps and diagrams are other visuals that can be used besides graphs. Prototyping is better suited for prescriptive/predictive models whereas graphs are a good way to represent descriptive analytics.

Apart from these basic principles on visualizations, analysts should be well versed in the design concepts and frameworks for visualization. For example, a good visualization might include 6 core principles from Gestalts' theory of design: proximity, similarity, enclosure, closure, continuity, and connection.

2.4.5 Document and Communicate Findings from Completed Analysis

When documenting and communicating the findings from an analytics initiative, analysts let the data drive the conclusions. Any conclusion reached should be based on the data collected; let the data speak for itself. Document and Communicate Findings from Completed Analysis includes identifying how to best package and communicate the data analysis results, making decisions about the level of summarization required, and grouping information for optimal understanding.

Analysts highlight the main themes, synthesizing results to build a narrative that can be understood by the intended recipients. Depending on the communication needs of the stakeholders, they may also produce reports and analytics dashboards.

Some questions to consider when reporting results are:

- What are the most important aspects of the conclusions for each stakeholder?
- Is there a graph or other form of visual representation that can communicate the information more effectively?
- What method of communication is going to be most effective to display the results in a meaningful way?
- Is there a way to make the communication more engaging (for example, a video or dynamic visualization rather than a pure text report)?

The findings include the results as well as an explanation of the methods used in the analysis, the process followed to derive the results, and any limitations or weaknesses in the data or methods used. When building the narrative, questions such as "Where are the data gaps?", "What does this mean for the business?", and "How can the business improve?" are addressed.

Data visualization uses visual models to communicate data relationships and results. The objective is to visually communicate information that is too complex to convey effectively in textual form. Through data visualization, tools, static graphs, and charts can be turned into dynamic models that decision-makers can use to view resulting analytics information from different perspectives and level of granularity.

Data storytelling involves the development of a narrative around the results of data analysis using patterns, trends, and behaviours observed. Stories are intended to create engagement so that stakeholders feel invested in the insights that are discovered. Data stories provide context to the situation being investigated through analytics with the objective of providing supporting information for organizational decision-making. Depending on the setting and mode of presentation, multiple techniques such as storyboards, elevator pitch, 3-minute story, the big idea, data journeys, and orchestration can be used to create the data stories.

It is here that the fundamental value proposition for business data analytics is demonstrated as the organization replaces its decision-making process based on instinct with one that is built on evidence-based decision-making. Data storytelling and data visualization work together to enable clear, concise, and visually appealing communication. These techniques are best performed by those who are visual thinkers and have effective communication skills.

2.4.6 Select Techniques for Interpret and Reporting Results

The following is a selection of some commonly used analysis and analytics techniques applicable to the Interpret and Report Results domain. The following list of techniques does not represent a comprehensive set of techniques used by an analyst in the Interpreting and Reporting Results domain but presents a small, but useful, set of techniques that can be used.

Techniques	Usage Context for Business Data Analytics	*BABOK® Guide v3.0* Reference
Interviews	Used to understand specific needs and expectations from stakeholders with respect to visualizations and communication.	Chapter 10.25
Prototyping	Used to systematically walk-through the analytics process to highlight certain conclusions. Prototyping is especially useful in predictive and prescriptive analytics settings.	Chapter 10.36
Root Cause Analysis	Used to organize various insights in such a way that explains a particular business phenomenon.	Chapter 10.40
Stakeholder List, Map, or Personas	Used to understand stakeholder needs and determine the visualization and communication requirements.	Chapter 10.43
Workshops	Used to distill multiple insights generated throughout the analytics life cycle to a set of business-relevant insights.	Chapter 10.50
Storyboarding	Used to communicate complex visualization or analytics approaches to stakeholders.	Chapter 11.1 The Agile Perspective
3-minute Story	Used to communicate insights to stakeholders in the form of a short business narrative.	N/A
Business Visualizations	Used to derive and communicate insights in simple and easy to understand charts, graphs, infographics, audio-visuals, and so forth. Business visualizations are meant to be simple representations for the consumption of stakeholders.	N/A
Data Journeys and Orchestration	Used to connect the entire data analysis journey and various decision points and analytics steps involved in the discovery process in the form of a visual hierarchy.	N/A

Techniques	Usage Context for Business Data Analytics	*BABOK® Guide v3.0* Reference
The Big Idea	Used to communicate the most relevant findings in a succinct manner. For example, if a visualization shows an S -Curve between marketing expense and the revenue generated by a cohort of customers, the big idea answers the "so -what" question, that is "beyond a certain dollar value marketing expense does not have any impact on revenue."	N/A
UX Patterns or Frameworks for Data Visualization	Used to design the visuals and stories using a distinct UX framework or best practices used in the enterprise.	N/A

2.4.7 A Case Study for Interpret and Report Results

HiFive Ice Creams is a premium ice cream retailer, with a strong urban presence and dozens of ice cream parlours in several major cities. HiFive implemented a new offering called "mix-ins" which they describe as a "create your own ice cream" concept. Customers have the ability to select from available ingredients, which are mixed into their ice cream resulting in a unique and customized flavour experience based on the selected ingredients.

HiFive executives routinely relied upon social media to connect with their customers and had used it to fuel brand recognition and brand experience. They attributed much of the company's success to their creative use of social media. To maximize the results of deploying their limited marketing budget, the ice cream retailer had decided to measure the success of its social media marketing efforts and created an appropriate approach.

.1 The Data Team's Work

The retailer developed a unique strategy to measure social media return on investment (ROI) and word-of-mouth value. A data team, including marketing sciences experts, data scientists, and business data analytics experts, was assembled. The team created an automated model that predicted the monetary value of social media marketing spend based on HiFive's objectives. The underlying framework for the automated model included a couple of unique metrics. Influence (IE), was developed to measure the net influence wielded by a user in a social network and predicted that user's ability to generate the spread of viral information. An additional metric, influence value (IV), measured the associated word-of-mouth linked to the actual sales that it generated.

Additionally, HiFive developed a process that helped them measure, monitor, and aggregate the data supplied by these metrics. Particular attention was focused on trends and analyzing the results. Over time, a strategy was developed that refined marketing activities to increase IE and IV, thereby positively impacting profit.

.2 Acquisition Proposal

Nine months into this process, HiFive was going through an acquisition bid from a global brand. Prisha Singhal, Director of Marketing from the acquiring organization, discovered this data while reviewing HiFive's strategic marketing plans. It sparked her interest and she decided to directly connect with the team. She was intrigued by the first three steps in this strategy where the team decided that Facebook would be the ideal social network, collecting very specific data and implementing a rewards program for influencers. Specifically, Prisha reached out to the team asking why Facebook was selected.

.3 Data Team's Response

The data science team responded that based on their study, they found Facebook has the highest regional adoption, which was conducive to the research problem. For this reason, they selected Facebook as the optimal medium.

Media	Example	Regional Adoption (#)	Proportion of Local Connection
Blogs	WordPress	37,590	13
Location Sharing	Foursquare	3,100	43
Personal Network	Facebook	64,000	57
Video Blog	YouTube	3,860	12
Micro Blog	Twitter	5,620	29
Virtual World	SecondLife	800	31
Social Coupons	Groupon	__	85

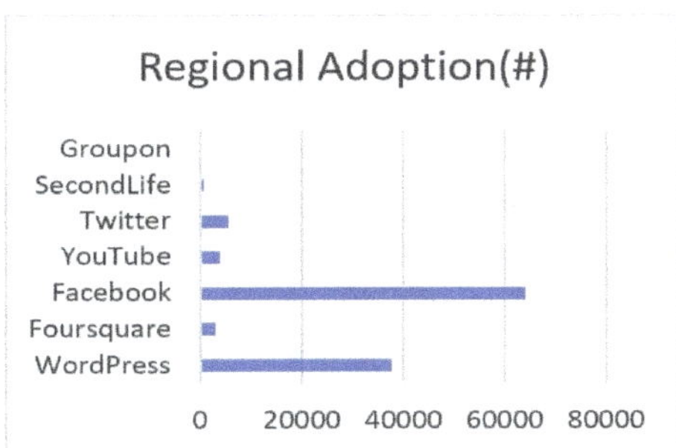

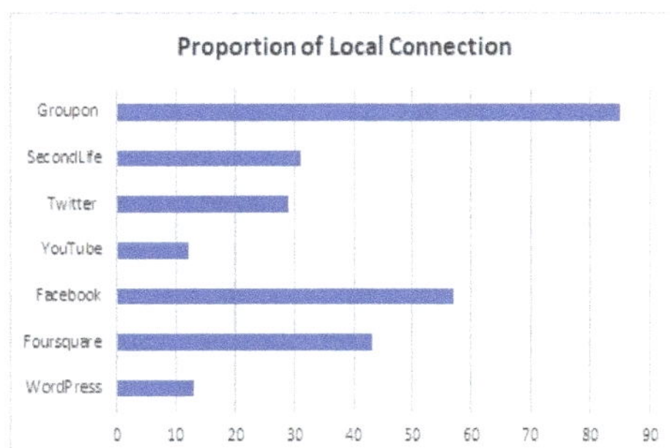

.4 The Challenge

Prisha was not convinced by this analysis, since it did not clearly justify how the data supports the strategic objective. She asked for additional clarification.

.5 Business Data Analytics Perspective

Chiran Varma is one of the business data analytics professionals on the team and he stepped in after hearing about this exchange between Prisha and the team. He took the following actions:

1. Chiran completed a quick stakeholder analysis to plan the communication needs for Prisha. Since Prisha is a significant influencer,

Chiran concluded that a more active and transparent communication approach is needed
2. Based on that, Chiran requested a meeting to discuss the entire approach and answer any additional questions Prisha may have.
3. He provided the team's background analysis to answer Prisha's question.
4. Chiran realized the information shared with Prisha was inadequate and not at the right level of detail.
5. Chiran knew there were a lot of background details that helped formulate the Facebook decision. He summarized this information and focused on the foundational analysis criteria which could be communicated as simply as possible.
6. Although graphs and tables are great for summarizing information, Chiran knew they need to be clearly communicated.

.6 Outcomes Achieved

Chiran built a simple decision matrix to illustrate why Facebook was chosen (depicted below) provided a clear explanation of how the criteria were relevant for the decision.

Decision Criteria	WordPress	Foursquare	Facebook	YouTube	Twitter	SecondLife	Groupon
Large number of users in a specific locality for a platform greater than 15,000	Yes		Yes				n/a
Percentage of social media contacts within the locality for a user greater than 25%		Yes	Yes		Yes	Yes	Yes
Effort required to share the message must be low		Yes	Yes		Yes	Yes	
Ease of creating connections to share the message must be simple			Yes	Yes	Yes	Yes	
Total	1	2	***4***	1	3	3	1

During the subsequent meeting, Chiran reviewed the table and the analysis with Prisha. He made a point of addressing every one of her concerns. Chiran's approach worked and Prisha came away with a solid understanding and a very favourable assessment of the team's work.

.7 Key Takeaways

- Interpreting and reporting results involves translation of the insights into a form that is easily understood by the stakeholders. The outcome of a technical analysis often points to a key fact. A translation of the facts into business relevant insight is needed. In this case, the graphs were translated into a format that is best suited for decision-making.
- One of the key activities in interpreting and reporting results involves communicating in such a way that the results are conveyed at the right level of detail. In this case, a business data analytics expert leveraged stakeholder analysis to focus on the most important information for a key stakeholder.

2.5 Use Results to Influence Business Decision-Making

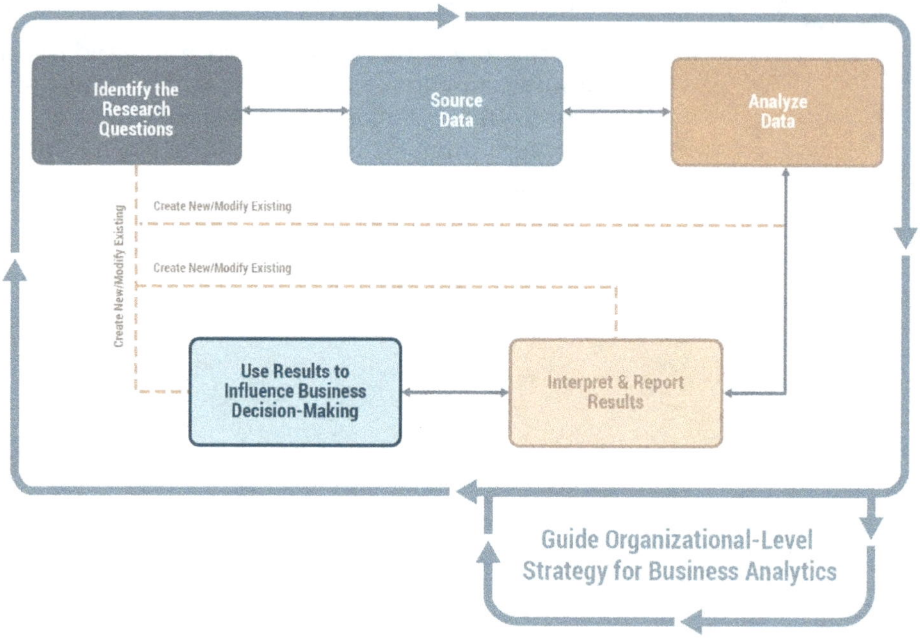

The Use Results to Influence Business Decision-Making domain involves using the analytics results to enable decision-making that generates value for the organization. Standalone reports and analytics results are useful only when some action is taken based on the insights that address the business problems or opportunities. Analytics results can be used as a strategic asset to influence the business model and processes. These results can be used both as decision support or by integrating into workflows to provide real-time decisions. For example, they can provide product recommendations in e-commerce, automated underwriting, fraud detection, and automated portfolio re-balancing in financial sectors.

Analysts translate the analytics outcomes to business recommendations that the stakeholders and decision-makers can consume. Analysts may be further required to develop a strategy on how the analytics results can be best used. Any business action that is influenced by the result of analytics initiative may result in an organizational change that affects people, process, offerings, or technology. This resulting change needs to be managed, and analysts are well suited for developing a plan that outlines how the transition can occur from the current state to a future state.

Tasks in the Use Results to Influence Business Decision-Making domain include:

- Recommend Actions,
- Develop Implementation Plan, and
- Manage Change.

2.5.1 Recommend Actions

Before an analyst can recommend changes to address the business need, an evaluation is conducted to determine the success of the analysis. Did the outcome of the analytics answer the research question? How well did the analysis address the business need?

The activities performed within the six domains of business data analytics are iterative. When the outcome is not what was expected, or if the data does not deliver the kind of insights required and there is no feasible solution that has been ascertained to address the business need, the business data analytics cycle is repeated, starting with the formation of a new research question.

If the analysis was enough to provide valuable insights to drive business change, the effort switches to using the results to drive conversations about how the changes will be made and implemented. These possibilities are referred to as solution options. Solution options proposed may include elements of the process, tool, resource, or IT system changes.

Analysts elicit the types of solution options the business might consider in addressing the business need, rating and ranking the options, and proposing a recommendation to the decision-makers based on the analysis and insights gleaned from the analytics efforts.

Business analysis professionals are skilled at identifying solutions that:

- align to the strategic direction of the organization,
- are valuable,
- provide a return for the needed investment, and
- address stated KPIs.

The ability to translate results of validated data analysis into solutions is typically an area where data professionals require support to make the connection back to the business. Business analysis professionals make the analytics results accessible to stakeholders and integrate them into deployable solutions.

Changes resulting from a business data analytics initiative are prioritized, funded, and initiated like other change proposals within the organization. Analysts play an important role in explaining the options and initiating the work required to move forward on making the recommended changes.

When recommending solution options, analysts use financial analysis techniques to determine the potential value of the various options. Focus groups are used to obtain feedback from participants with regards to the options under consideration. Other types of models, whether they are depicting processes, scope, or various elements of the organization, are used when making a recommendation or explaining a solution. Creative thinking, problem-solving, and systems and conceptual thinking are all skills used by analysts when recommending actions.

Example of Integrating Predictive Analytics Results to Business Workflow

A large e-commerce retailer updates the pricing of their products dynamically. Customer experience and trust are significant equity for any large scale retailer. With millions of pricing updates taking place in the e-commerce platform for millions of products, any pricing anomalies can result in loss of customers. Anomaly detection algorithms that can mitigate the issue in real-time can be a true game-changer. This type of algorithm can work on various types of data such as competitor prices, historical product prices, delivery cost, in-store prices, and discounts to arrive at estimated product prices that can then be used as a reference to detect anomalous pricing. An analytics initiative can detect anomalous pricing of the product in order to identify pricing deviations that result from incorrect data input.

Consider a predictive analytics proof of concept to detect pricing anomalies with a mix of models, for example, Gaussian Naïve Bayes, autoencoders, gradient boost, and random forest. The evaluation criterion is the F1 score, which minimizes both false positive and false negatives simultaneously. The performance of this combination could satisfactorily classify a pricing update as an anomaly or not, with acceptable results for use by business stakeholders. The proof of concept uses static data from various data sources to produce the results. In this scenario the analytics solution was very technical. Business analysis professionals require understanding the technical aspects at just enough depth to assess the solution against business needs. More importantly, a business analysis professional performs additional analysis to determine whether the analytics solution can be integrated with the current processes. Analytics results alone are not sufficient to deploy the solution and requires more analysis.

When recommending such a solution, analysts consider:

- What is the financial return on investment of the solution when deployed in a production environment? For example, deployment cost that may involve live data streams and unstructured data collection, new solution architecture, future implementation costs, changes to the already complex pricing algorithms versus the savings from incorrect pricing, and some quantifiable metric that allows a clear comparison between the costs and the benefits.
- Are there any alternative solutions? For example, could a different analytics model be deployed with a lower cost implication; if the new prices are some standard deviation away from the old price, is it an anomaly?
- What processes change if the solution is deployed? Will there be a real-time blocking on the purchases if prices are determined to be an anomaly? When should the new predictive analytics algorithms be deployed—during pricing loads, item purchase, or for product categories as a batch? Should the high-priced items be prioritized?
- How will the deployed solution behave? For example, what is the new data architecture, and how does it fit in with other impacted solutions such as product recommendations?

2.5.2 Develop Implementation Plan

An implementation plan outlines the implementation strategy and includes a road map of the changes and tasks that must be completed to ensure the successful implementation of a change. Implementation plans for an analytics initiative are no different than implementation plans for other types of initiatives.

The implementation plan includes tasks, sub-tasks, resources, and high-level estimates provided by the stakeholders responsible for completing the tasks and a sequence showing flow and task dependencies. Constraints, assumptions, risks, and dependencies are also identified and discussed.

When developing an implementation plan, analysts break down the work to implement the proposed changes. Functional decomposition is a technique that is used to drill down high-level tasks into lower-level tasks and activities. This often takes the form of a work breakdown structure or story maps. Brainstorming, and a variety of elicitation techniques, are used to identify an initial list of tasks for the plan. Skills in facilitation to lead planning discussions are helpful when developing an implementation plan.

2.5.3 Manage Change

Change originating out of an analytics initiative may be managed by a change management team, which analysts support, or analysts may hold the role of change manager. In this role they oversee the transformation of the analysis results into implemented policies and procedures within the organization. Implementing change is the end goal and it is where the organization realizes the value from its analytics efforts.

Business analysts are well suited in fulfilling the role of change manager as they are able to ensure the continuity between the analytics work and implementation. Before implementing changes, stakeholders agree on what changes to make. Similar to other types of projects, there is a level of effort required to analyze the options and understand the constraints, risks, assumptions, costs, and value proposition for each option before a decision can be made on the type of change to be implemented. Analysts play an important role in facilitating discussions, explaining options, and driving the decision-making process.

When managing change, analysts use various types of models to communicate existing processes and workflows. The same models can be used to show proposed changes. Organization models, process models, and sequence diagrams are some of these models. Systems thinking skills are helpful in understanding the people, processes, and technologies. Analysts also provide information on how best to make changes that are based on analytics results. Analysts leverage teaching skills effectively to communicate proposed procedural changes. Decision-making skills aid in facilitating agreements on the types of changes to be made.

2.5.4 Select Techniques for Use Results to Influence Business Decision-Making

The following is a selection of some commonly used analysis and analytics techniques applicable to the Use Results to Influence Decision-Making domain. The following list of techniques does not represent a comprehensive set of techniques used by an analyst in the Use Results to Influence Decision-Making domain but presents a small, but useful, set of techniques that can be used.

Techniques	**Usage Context for Business Data Analytics**	***BABOK® Guide* v3.0 Reference**
Acceptance and Evaluation Criteria	Used for evaluating recommendations from analytics against agreed-upon acceptance criteria and the alignment with the business need.	Chapter 10.1
Balanced Scorecard	Used for assessing organizational impact by implementing recommended actions or any alternate solution.	Chapter 10.3
Benchmarking and Market Analysis	Used to evaluate competitor and market reactions if certain recommendations from the analytics initiative are implemented.	Chapter 10.4
Decision Analysis	Used to understand and assess the recommendations and alignment of recommendation to business problems. Multiple tools such as decision trees, multi-factor analysis, and sensitivity analysis can be performed to evaluate the recommendations.	Chapter 10.16
Financial Analysis	Used to evaluate financial performance when recommended actions or alternate solutions are implemented.	Chapter 10.20
Lessons Learned	Used to compile the learnings from the analytics initiative with respect to improvements that can be made to the analytics approach, data resources, analytics capabilities, and organizational capabilities that can be leveraged for future initiatives.	Chapter 10.27
Organizational Modelling	Used to assist change management where the organizational model is being impacted.	Chapter 10.32
Prioritization	Used to prioritize recommendations or solution options arising out of analytics initiative.	Chapter 10.33
Process Analysis	Used to understand the impact of recommendations on the future state of business processes.	Chapter 10.34
Risk Analysis and Management	Used to assess associated risks, constraints, and dependencies by implementing a solution approach or initiating any change.	Chapter 10.38

2.5.5 A Case Study for Use Results to Influence Business Decision-Making

The UK giftware and online gifting industry has gone through unprecedented changes in recent years. Retailers in this industry are experiencing cost pressures and need to increase effective marketing practices in the crowded and historically seasonal marketplace. To differentiate in this highly competitive environment, several top retailers are investing in more customized gift offerings that are personalized for newer target market segments.

.1 The Challenge

The giftware industry regularly transitions through seasonal high-demand and low-demand cycles throughout the calendar year, attributed to various influencing factors. Special occasions such as birthdays, family events (such as engagements, graduations, or weddings), and corporate events are a continuous source of revenue for the giftware industry. However, the major revenue has always been from holiday seasons like Christmas.

GiftRonline is a UK-based and registered non-store online retail company. The company mainly sells unique all-occasion gifts. Considering these aspects, GiftRonline has determined that new market segments are needed for accurate targeting than the traditional demographic segments that they have used in the past. GiftRonline has provided transactional sales data for a year to their data science team to evaluate the possibility of new segments. The data consisted of invoice details such as stock code, product description, customer identifier, unit price, ordered quantity, and delivery country of each invoice or online purchase for a year.

The data science team debated the best analytics approach to use based on the large data set they received. They considered several approaches for segmentation, including value-based segmentation, recency-frequency-monetary analysis (RFM), and psychographic segmentation. After considerable time and effort and with the help of David Brown, a business analysis professional on their team, they settled on the approach to use.

.2 Analytics Approach

The team decided to:

- review product descriptions and group them into specific product baskets,
- resolve overlapping products into single product baskets, and
- cluster customers based on their propensity to buy specific product groups or basket value'

This analytics approach was carried out by extracting keywords from product descriptions (for example, jewelry) and creating distinct product groups, then to distribute customers, based on buying patterns into a specific product group. Analyzing this data, the data science team communicated the following results:

- Five product groupings or categories were identified, and customers were segregated into eleven clusters based on these product categories.
- New customers could be classified into the right cluster with almost (75%) accuracy using an optimized clustering model.

.3 Management Reaction

GiftsRonline executives were satisfied with the collaboration and communication between the business and the analytics team but were confused about how best to proceed. In particular, they were unsure about how to leverage this data to meet their original objectives. They had the following key questions:

- What are the product and customer segments and how best to describe their characteristics? Future marketing strategies will revolve around deeper understanding of these segments. The current groupings simply label the segments as cluster no.0, cluster no.1, and so forth.
- How do we operationalize results into the current business? For example, based on these categories are there any recommendations that stand out?

.4 Outcomes Achieved

Additional analysis was completed as David determined how best to communicate this data, and the analytics team was asked to create some key visualizations.

1. The team produced a word cloud to demonstrate new product category identifiers.

   Keywords were extracted from product descriptions within a category:

   David used the word cloud to highlight and recommend easily understandable cluster names to best describe the product categories.

For example, cluster no.2 contains products associated with "Holiday crafts" and cluster no.4 was renamed "Jewelry & Luxury".

The team then cross-referenced product categories with item values and delivery information for a more refined description of each product category. These were used to help key stakeholders understand product and customer segments.

2. The team produced spider chart visualizations to clearly differentiate segments.

This chart described each customer segment with individual axes as categories and included attributes such as count (number of purchase visits), mean (average price paid per order), and sum (average spend per customer):

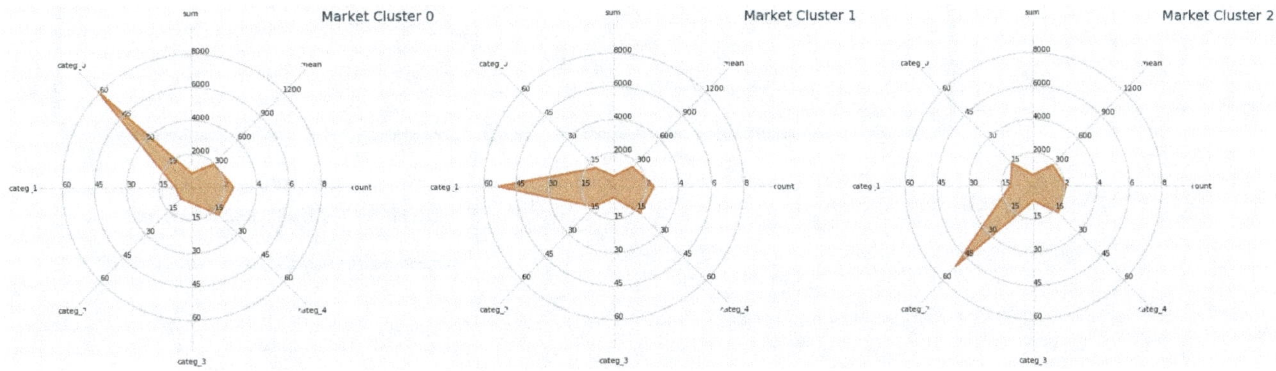

Note: for simplicity, this diagram only depicts the first three categories out of 11.

From the visual it could be clearly deduced that each customer segment has a distinct propensity towards a product group, which validated the findings and the analytical approach.

3. To operationalize these findings, David conducted a feasibility study to integrate the analytics finding with the GiftRonline CRM application and provided recommendation aligned to the new marketing segments.

.5 Key Takeaways

- Data insights can influence business decisions, but those insights need to be effectively communicated. The starting point is to develop a shared understanding of analytics results and insights from those results. By leveraging business analysis techniques, the analytics team was able to:
  - Effectively communicate the outcomes of the analytics work.
  - Develop a shared understanding of what the data was demonstrating.
  - Use their insights to influence decision-making.

2.6 Guide Organizational-Level Strategy for Business Data Analytics

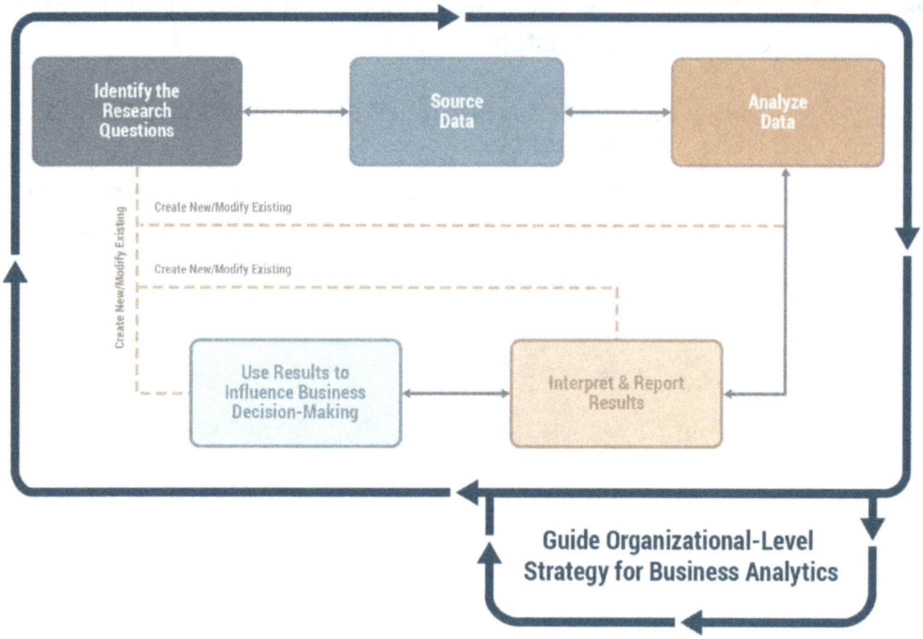

The success of analytics engagements depends on the organizations disposition to analytics. Business data analytics provides the transformational capabilities for guiding organizations to be analytics-driven.

The Guide Organizational-Level Strategy for Business Data Analytics domain builds on the first five domains that describe a business data analytics practitioner's work by elaborating on organizational elements that support their success.

Organizations obtain valuable insights from data and these insights support informed business decision-making. Organizations invest in analytics to deliver on their strategic imperatives to innovate and obtain competitive advantages in the marketplace. These investments drive the demand for more skilled professionals with business data analytics knowledge and experience.

The Guide Organizational-Level Strategy for Business Data Analytics domain explores how organizations can embed analytics initiatives into the organizational architecture and overall decision-making framework. This domain describes about how organizations can be transformed and made more conducive to being data- and insights-powered.

Task in the Guide Organizational-Level Strategy for Business Data Analytics domain include:

- Organizational Strategy,
- Talent Strategy, and
- Data Strategy.

2.6.1 Organizational Strategy

Organizations aiming to integrate analytics to drive business decisions consider unique organizational models for the analytics team and how these organizational models can be situated within the organization in relation to other teams and business units. Many organizations start with analytics initiatives as proof of concepts or pilots for projects that have a limited impact on the strategic posture of the organization.

The following organizational models can help with a transformation from an analytics-aware organization to an analytics-driven organization.

- ***Centralized*** model refers to the analytics team operating as a single unit supporting other business units in decision- making. An analytics Centre of Excellence is a good example of a centralized model where upskilling talent may be an advantage as it forms a cohesive team within the organizational structure.

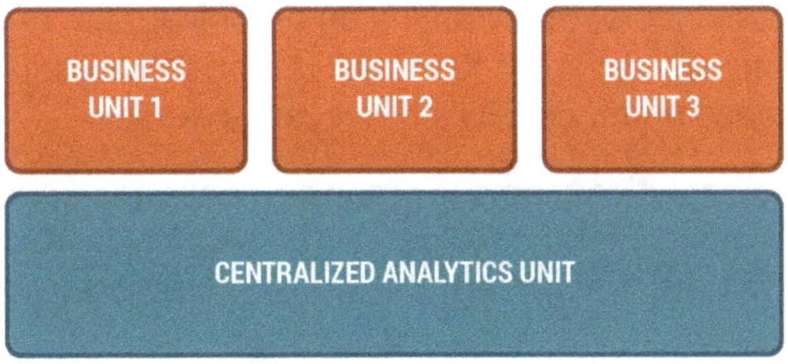

- ***Decentralized*** model refers to the model where analytics teams are embedded in different business units. In a decentralized model, analytics teams may be more aligned to the business practices and processes of a business unit which may positively influence specialized analytics solutions within that business unit.

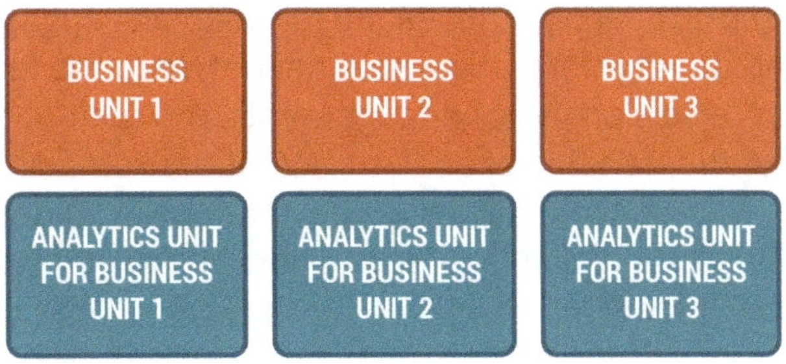

- ***Hybrid*** model refers to a mix of centralized and decentralized analytics teams operating within an organization. For example, a hub and spoke model can be considered with geographic separation for hubs and centralized structure within a specific geography to structure the analytics teams.

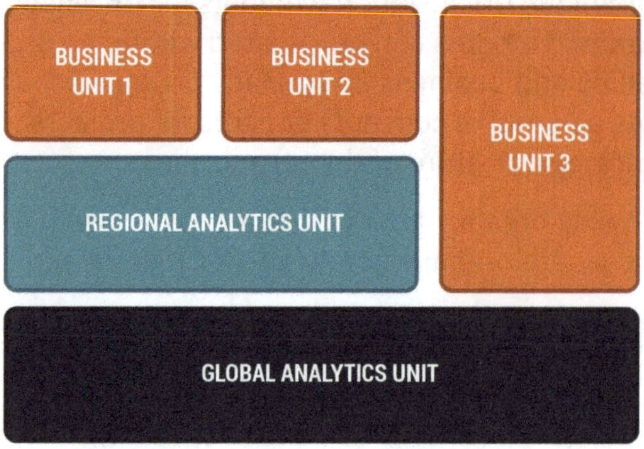

Another choice of determining an organizational model for analytics teams is to organize by different functions within the organization such as business intelligence units, IT, CIO's office, an so forth.

How the analytics teams is organized depends upon, but is not limited to:

- enterprise data ownership,
- governance within the organization,
- requirements around outsourcing the analytics,
- competition,
- overall industry outlook,
- supplier and vendor relationships, and
- involvement of senior leadership in analytics efforts.

Analytics teams are most effective when they are cross-functional. Executive leadership support is a necessity for analytics engagements to succeed. A clear and direct information channel between the leadership and analytics teams to review analytics engagements and their outcomes ensures there is a shared understanding of analytic activities. Some organizations that have had success with analytic initiatives have adopted an organization model for analytics teams which is directly under the executive leadership of Chief Analytics Officer.

When determining the right organizational model for analytics teams, multiple strategic business analysis skills are used to connect enterprise components with analytics. Systems thinking, conceptual thinking, and expertise in collaborating with cross-functional stakeholders, including executive leadership, all help define organizational models. Techniques such as business model canvas, balanced scorecard, benchmarking and market analysis, value chain analysis, SWOT, and CATWOE are relevant in connecting enterprise components for analytics transformation.

A Sample Organization of Analytics Teams within a Large Organization

Building an effective model for the analytics team depends on various organizational components such as business functions, leadership oversight, existing data architecture and sources, and types of business data. Many organizations start with a decentralized approach for analytics engagements with analytics embedded into different business units. With maturity in data governance, data best practices within an organization start to leverage analytics for strategic benefits. The organizational model may reflect maturity over time. For large scale enterprises, the analytics team takes either a hybrid or a centralized shape with multiple business units requesting parallel engagements from the analytics organization with standardized practice.

An example of a Centre of Excellence for analytics may resemble a model such as this:

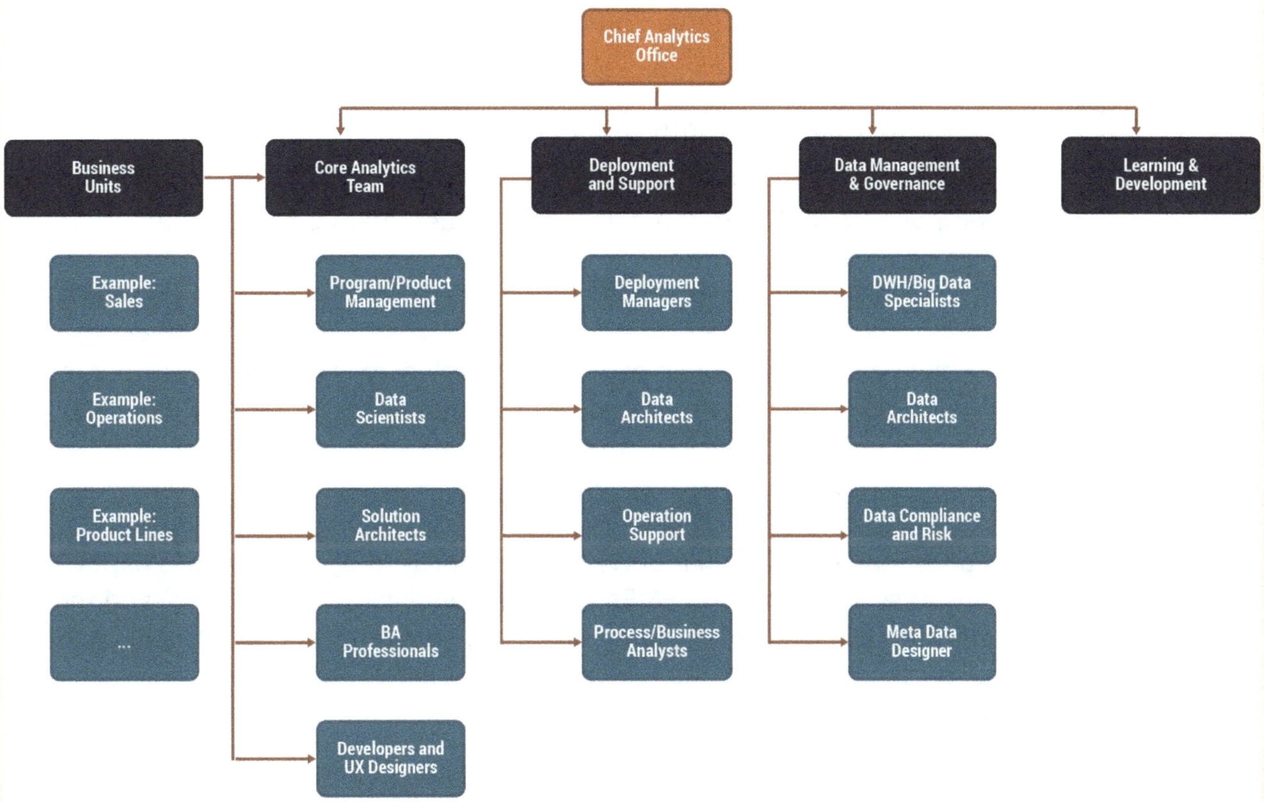

2.6.2 Talent Strategy

With the growing demand for analytics professionals, organizations create an strategy to attract and retain analytics professionals and related roles. Competitive compensation is one of the main driving factors in the industry. Several other factors also contribute to recruiting and retaining analytics professionals:

- opportunity to work on engaging and exciting initiatives,
- ability to work directly with key decision-makers,
- opportunity to learn the business,
- ability to solve complex business problems,
- access to relevant tools and technologies, and
- a culture that promotes trust and appreciation.

In addition to recruitment and retention of talent, there are three major components that form the pillars of a robust talent strategy at an organizaitonal level:

- establishing the right team structure for analytics initiatives,
- the ability to create an eco-system for learning and development, and
- establishing best practices for analytics initiatives.

.1 Team Structure for Analytics Initiatives

A productive partnership between those providing the business experience (business stakeholders, SMEs, business analysis professionals) and those with the technical skills (data engineers, data analysts, scientists) contribute to the success of any data-driven engagement. These roles work collaboratively to ensure the business context is properly translated to guide the analytics activities appropriately and to find the best ways to obtain value from available data.

For a large organization, the analytics team structure may consist of any or all of the following roles:

- ***Subject matter experts (SMEs)***: provide specific knowledge of the business sector or specified business domain (for example, finance and human resources).
- ***Data/solution architect***: designs and develops data systems to capture and store data. Generally, does not program systems as that is the role of the data engineer.
- ***Data engineer***: develops and maintains data systems.
- ***Data scientist***: applies advanced technical skills to create and evaluate analytics models to obtain insights from data.
- ***Data analyst***: interprets and analyzes data; may work under the direction of the data scientist.

- ***Experience designer***: develops customized experience prototypes and visual enhancements for different levels of stakeholders that aids in communication and comprehension of analytics results.
- ***Data journalist***: turns results into data stories that can be communicated to different levels of stakeholders within the organization.
- ***Business analysis professional***: establishes the scope for the analytics work and utilizes results to support business decision-making and implementation of the resulting decisions.

The right team structure for analytics initiatives is guided by the organization's capabilities. Capabilities in business data analytics enable practitioners to play multiple roles within analytics initiatives.

Each of these roles has overlapping and complementary skills. Based on the organization's needs, and criteria such as the size of the initiative, the industry, budget, project plan, and organizational capabilities, multiple roles can be merged to create the right team structure. For example, a business analysis professional with sufficient analytics and business knowledge can play the roles of SME, data analyst, and data journalist, and support data architecture, data engineering, and experience design. The focus area for an organization-level strategy is primarily to determine the guidelines that govern the right team structure for the right initiative.

.2 Learning and Development for Talent Strategy

The complexity of analytics capabilities is changing at an extremely rapid pace, from data management technologies that are capable of handling large volume with high velocity and variety to analytics platforms and toolsets that include complex machine learning and deep learning architectures. Analytics objectives have evolved to be able to include predictive and prescriptive objectives with data science, machine learning, and artificial intelligence playing a increasing role.

To address this rapid transformation, organizations formulate strategies to continuously upgrade their talent in emerging analytics platforms and workbench, big data, and cloud technologies. Many such platforms and technologies are offered an open source, self-service, and codeless forms. For example, Microsoft Azure ML service offers visual modelling for machine learning, which can be used by business professionals directly with a minimal amount of coding. Google's TensorFlow packages help build complex neural networks with a great deal of accuracy. Hadoop/Spark packages manage large unstructured data and create data lakes that can hold a vast amount of raw data.

In addition to the technical competencies and analytics platforms knowledge, key attributes that ensure analytics success are strong business knowledge and the ability to understand the underlying statistical and mathematical concepts. Many of the analytics solutions in predictive and prescriptive spaces are dependent on the business problem that requires custom analytical models. Strong business and mathematical foundations are essential competencies for analytics solutions.

Communicating the findings in the right way, by developing data stories and visuals, is equally critical to ensure the business outcome. Even if the analytics initiative is producing quality results, if the results are not understood by the stakeholders the entire engagement could be at risk.

When formulating a learning and development strategy, organizations focus on business knowledge, technology and analytics platforms, and data communication and translation competency areas.

.3 Establishing Best Practices

Best practices in analytics engagements are established through the accumulation of experience, lessons learned, and current knowledge and advancements in industry trends. Knowledge about other industries also helps in establishing the best practices.

Establishing best practices in analytics involves identifying a standard set of tools and techniques that work well for the organization, for the types of problems being solved, and for the skill sets and capabilities available. Best practices that provide a set of standard procedures can be recommended to be adopted by organization-wide analytics teams. For example, in establishing best practices, an organization may develop policies to ensure sampling methods between different analytics projects are shared across teams.

Another best practice is maintaining subsets of analytics requirements for re-use or establishing a procedure for securing approval for data access. Whatever the practice is, the motivation for identifying, stating, and developing policies around best practices is to shape analytics in a way that fosters improved performance and moves the organization forward to obtain more value from the investments being made in these initiatives.

2.6.3 Data Strategy

Organization-level strategy guides comprehensive analytics engagements managing data residing within and outside the organization. Simply consolidating organizational data for a single analytics initiative may be sufficient for organizations that are interested in achieving ad hoc results. Unplanned analytics initiatives with a weak data strategy can only provide limited business value.

Organizations with large scale analytics engagements consider how data is acquired, stored, and used in a planned way. Multiple components influence the data strategy, including end-to-end enterprise data architecture, storage capabilities, data privacy, and data governance policies driving data life cycle within the organization. As more and more data sources start residing outside the control of the analytics team within the organization, policies directing the data integrity, consistency, relevancy, and other quality parameters are established.

Similarly, data gateways from devices such as the internet of things (IoT), sensors, business applications, and business processes are established for data storage in cloud environments. When the volume and velocity of data acquisitions increase, as in the case of streaming data, or the number of analytics initiatives increase within the organization, keeping track of an organization's data and data requests becomes a complex activity. In the absence of a single source of truth, a just in time approach, or a self-service strategy can be employed to cater to data needs within the organization.

An organization-level data strategy may include the following planning considerations:

- ***Data governance***: the rules and policies that manage the data assets of an organization to ensure high-quality data.
- ***Data architecture***: the models and standards that govern how data is collected, stored, and integrated across an organization.
- ***Data security***: the activities performed to protect data from a privacy and confidentiality perspective.
- ***Metadata management***: the administration of information that is maintained about the data assets an organization collects and manages.

When formulating a data strategy for an organization, technical professionals take inventory of the existing environments. All planning considerations align with a strategic goal and a future state applicable to the organization. Business analysis professionals bring this strategic perspective to the forefront and collaborate with IT and the business to design an end-to-end strategy for data and analytics.

2.6.4 Select Techniques for Guide Organizational-Level Strategy for Business Data Analytics

The following is a selection of some commonly used analysis and analytics techniques applicable to the Organizational-Level Strategy for Business Data Analytics domain. The following list of techniques does not represent a comprehensive set of techniques used by an analyst in the Organizational-Level Strategy for Business Data Analytics domain but presents a small, but useful, set of techniques that can be used.

Techniques	Usage Context for Business Data Analytics	*BABOK® Guide* v3.0 Reference
Balanced Scorecard	Used to describe a balanced view of the organization from different perspectives. It is useful for aligning the data strategy to business objectives and outcomes.	Chapter 10.3
Benchmarking and Market Analysis	Use to identify problems and opportunities in the current state and plan for the future state to align the organizational-level strategy. Often used with with different frameworks such as Five Forces, STEEP, and CATWOE.	Chapter 10.4
Five Forces	Use to analyze the market forces that determine the effectiveness of analytics strategies. For example, it can be useful to evaluate new entrants that are heavily utilizing analytics in a particular industry.	Chapter 10.4 (Benchmarking and Market Analysis)
Business Capability Analysis	Used to create a hierarchical catalogue of capabilities the organizaion possesses and determine the role of analytics where it can enhance or restrict any business capabilities. For example, adding analytics for sales and marketing can enhance the ability of the teams to effectively target and communicate enterprise value propositions to the customers.	Chapter 10.6
Business Model Canvas	Used to understand how the organizaion creates value propositions and how analytics is currently leveraged. It is useful in identifying areas where analytics can be a competitive advantage in delivering business outcomes.	Chapter 10.8
Collaborative Games	Use to encourage stakeholders in an analytics strategy formulation activity to collaborate in building a joint understanding of the strategy.	Chapter 10.10
Metrics and Key Performance Indicators (KPIs)	Used to understand how analytics can influence the metrics and KPIs of an enterprise as well as the KPIs for analytics strategy once implemented.	Chapter 10.28
Organizational Modeling	Used to understand and identify gaps in the current organizational models to design the organization strategy for analytics.	Chapter 10.32

Techniques	Usage Context for Business Data Analytics	*BABOK® Guide* v3.0 Reference
Risk Analysis and Management	Used to identify and mitigate uncertainties in the analytics strategy for the enterprise. For example, it can be used to determine an alternate course of action when analytics engagements fail.	Chapter 10.38
SWOT Analysis	Used to understand the enterprise's strengths, weaknesses, opportunities, and threats. It is useful for explaining the internal and external context of an organization. For example, it can be used to assess how analytics can be used to mitigate the challenges or generate opportunities for the organization.	Chapter 10.46
Value Chain Analysis	Used to discover how value is added through key activities within the organization to deliver products and services to the customers. It is useful to outline the key business units where analytics can enhance the value of the offerings.	Chapter 10.6 (Business Capability Analysis)

2.6.5 Underlying Competencies for Guide Organizational-Level Strategy for Business Data Analytics

It is important to build a supportive organizational environment to drive the full value of business data analytics initiatives. This includes building relevant capabilities and leveraging best practices for data management at an organizational level. Business data analytics practitioners can help ensure appropriate discussions take place and effective practices are adopted. To achieve this, they will rely heavily on the following key underlying competencies.

Underlying Competencies	Usage Context for Organizational Strategy for Analytics	*BABOK® Guide* v3.0 Reference
Analytical Thinking and Problem Solving: • Creative Thinking • Decision Making • Systems Thinking • Conceptual Thinking	While creating and implementing an organizational level strategy for analytics, a business analysis professional can use these underlying competencies to: • Analyze various ideas and approaches to implement a specific strategy. • Assist in informed decision making based on various criteria and have an objective evaluation. • Think holistically about interactions between people, process and technological aspects to suggest a specific strategy. • Connect seemingly abstract, large, and potentially disparate information for arriving at a suitable strategy.	• Chapter 9.1 • Sub-section 9.1.1 • Sub-section 9.1.2 • Sub-section 9.1.5 • Sub-section 9.1.6
Business Knowledge: • Business Acumen • Industry Knowledge • Organization Knowledge • Solution Knowledge • Methodology Knowledge	While creating and implementing an organizational-level strategy for analytics, a business analysis professional can use these underlying competencies to: • Appreciate the importance of fundamental business principles and best practices across industries to review the organizational strategy. • Understand current practices and activities within an industry and similar processes across industries for organizational strategy. • Consider the management structure and business architecture of the enterprise while designing strategy. • Recommend various approaches based on technologies, analytics platforms, and future trends. • Develop an approach based on context, dependencies, opportunities, and constraints.	• Chapter 9.3 • Sub-section 9.3.1 • Sub-section 9.3.2 • Sub-section 9.3.3 • Sub-section 9.3.4 • Sub-section 9.3.5

Underlying Competencies	Usage Context for Organizational Strategy for Analytics	*BABOK® Guide* v3.0 Reference
Communication Skills	While creating and implementing an organizational-level strategy for analytics, a business analysis professional can use these underlying competencies to: • Gather as much information as possible through verbal and non-verbal cues. • Listen and understand abstract information. • Communicate clearly and precisely about the strategy across all the levels within the organization.	• Chapter 9.4
Interaction Skills	While creating and implementing an organizational-level strategy for analytics, a business analysis professional can use these underlying competencies to: • Facilitate interaction between multiple stakeholders involved in the initiative. • Resolve conflicts between various parties involved.	• Chapter 9.5

2.6.6 A Case Study for Guide Organization-Level Strategy for Business Data Analytics

Singapore has one of the oldest and most well-developed retirement programs in Asia, consisting of defined contribution plans in individual accounts. Mai Tan works as one of several product owners at Retire Inc., a young company that recently launched a new product, RetireSafe for the citizens of Singapore. RetireSafe allows qualified individuals to determine how prepared they are for retirement. RetireSafe verifies citizenship based on tax identification data and demographic details, allowing it to interact with government databases for publicly available data. It also allows individuals to enter employment details, current net worth, financial assets, health status, post retirement plans, and desired future income streams.

With this information identified, the product generates assessments and scenarios depicting what kind of retirement the individual can expect through an interactive, intuitive dashboard. Sensitivity analysis features are incorporated to allow individuals to modify parameters and see the impact of those changes. In this way, the product provides information to help citizens better understand and maximize the expected results for their individual accounts.

.1 An Overwhelming Success

RetireSafe was developed by Mai's team and has been available for approximately twelve months. It is both the company's largest investment in product development and is on track to becomes its highest generating product. RetireSafe has been warmly embraced by Singaporean citizens who have flooded the company with requests for new features and additional functionality. The product team adds each request to a product backlog where it is prioritized for upcoming releases. Mai uses several metrics to track performance and adoption of various product features. She also uses this information to decide which features to remove to reduce ongoing maintenance costs. Afterall, as a young organization, it's a constant challenge to ensure positive returns that can be used to fund building additional features.

To add greater depth in understanding adoption and customer satisfaction, Mai decided to track product usage and satisfaction indicators through a net promoter score (NPS) as a single high-level metric. She used several drill-down metrics, detailed information tracking feature usage, and time individuals spent constructing various types of scenarios to provide more clarity. This type of data helped the team assess and prioritize requested new features.

The product team has built and rolled out a steady stream of new features but is overwhelmed by requests. What was originally envisioned as an annual product release cycle has become a quarterly release from a team that has doubled in size since the initial launch of this product. Their work has become increasingly more difficult in the last few weeks as other Retire Inc.

departments have requested access to the information being collected through this product. Other teams want to use this data to build a repository of prospects, cross sell existing financial products, and design new or enhanced products. As busy as the product team is, Mai realizes her work is no longer just about rolling out new enhancements to a popular product.

.2 The Challenge

To continue its growth and success, Retire Inc. needs to holistically view how data is managed and governed on behalf of all interested stakeholders. Requests for data tracked by Mai's product team has identified issues that need to be resolved at an organization level. These include:

- Who decides which departments can have access to the data?
- How much data can be shared?
- What data should be restricted?
- How will data be secured as its shared?
- What other standards or policies need to be in place for data usage?
- Who in the organization enforces these data management procedures?
- How will Retire Inc. avoid inconsistent data silos cropping up?

Mai extended discussions beyond her team and helped inform other leaders about the way in which the product team uses data to drive their decision making. Other departments made a case for taking charge of and building similar data management expertise within their teams. With others seeing the benefits, and the request for data pouring in, Mai was asked to recommend how best to proceed. After some initial research, she decides to assess two basic options:

- advocate for a single focused analytics team (centralized function), or
- recommend analytics expertise be developed throughout Retire Inc. (decentralized function).

.3 Analyzing and Assessing

Mai relied on several business analysis techniques to build her understanding of what needs to be done, including: benchmarking, business capability analysis, organizational modelling, and SWOT analysis. Through her benchmarking analysis and discussions with other organizations that have greater data maturity, she learned about the importance of data architecture and data governance. It also helped her develop a clear picture of what future practices could look like. Using organizational modelling techniques, Mai developed a good understanding of where changes could be made in Retire Inc.'s current data practices and she recognized the shortfall in skills that are currently missing - those that are needed to effectively evolve data analytic practices. She also started to have appreciation for what the desired changes would cost and wondered how she could possibly secure the required budget to propose a centralized data analytics function. Mai's business capability analysis helped her identify areas of opportunities and components that could be leveraged as Retire Inc. continues this journey. She discovered that all the existing data expertise within Retire Inc. lies within her product team.

Her SWOT analysis helped strengthen her analysis and provided vital information to include in her assessment.

This assessment also solidified the important responsibility that Retire Inc. had to protect customer data. Mai realized that RetireSafe data included personally identifiable and sensitive information such as age, income and net worth which needed to be securely managed within internal departments. Formulating internal guidelines for use of this information, anonymizing it while still providing value, meeting General Data Protection Regulation (GDPR regulations, and meeting other government or financial regulations would require time and expertise.

Throughout this analysis, Mai used her knowledge of key stakeholders to share her findings, determine what Retire Inc. leaders really wanted, and identified potential sources of funding to support the future implementation of data analytics expertise. Although not an exhaustive list, Mai was able to summarize the pros and cons for her two basic options as follows:

Solution Options	Pros	Cons
Single focused analytics team ***(centralized)***	• Easier to establish data usage guidelines. • Easier to standardize data-related processes, templates, and metrics. • Easier to mange a data governance framework. • Provide greater consistency across Retire Inc. • Data capability uplift through easier sharing of experiences. • Easier to deploy data management standards. • Better able to identify data usage opportunities across Retire Inc. • Easier to develop data capabilities.	• Data related expertise only exists in one key group. • May encounter problems identifying the research questions and communicating the results as they are more detached from stakeholders. • Processes, methods, and approaches may be perceived as cumbersome. • Retire Inc. staff may perceive a greater sense of bureaucracy. • May impede agility with more Retire Inc. staff having more hurdles to meet. • More challenging to identify who should be involved in helping develop organization data standards. • Lack of flexibility and agility for adhoc reports and insights - this team will be constrained by current standards. • May take longer to meet departmental needs for specific data. • May slow down departmental-level decision making.
Analytics expertise throughout Retire Inc. ***(decentralized)***	• Data expertise is developed throughout Retire Inc. • Retire Inc. staff help create data-related standards. • Data governance and data usage standards may be more readily embraced. • More flexibility and agility in managing requests for analytics. • Greater diversity in how Retire Inc. makes use of data. • Greater flexibility in choosing tools, approaches, and methods to address specific data-related challenges.	• Consistency of data governance and data usage standards. • Data quality issues may arise. • May impact consistency of decision-making. • Risk of siloed data that is of little use to other departments at Retire Inc. • Increase in talent-related costs, both acquisition and ongoing development.

.4 Recommendation

Based on her analysis, Mai realized it wasn't a binary option. She recommended establishing data standards within the RetireSafe team, specifically around data sharing and light-weight data governance practices. As the organization gained better understanding of their data needs, Mai recommended they transition to a centralized analytics function sourcing some members from the RetireSafe team and augmenting them with key personal to account for deficiencies in key skillsets. In the meantime, she recommended carefully adding data experts to the RetireSafe team through short term contracts to help mature data architecture practices.

.5 Rationale

Both centralizing and decentralizing in themselves would be helpful but the advantages or disadvantages are finely balanced. There were not enough benefits for either option to merit one over the other. Other criteria proved to be instrumental in Mai's recommendation. Particularly the need to mature data management practices, align with budget considerations and the ability to move fast.

Retire Inc. is a new company with an "in demand" product that is demanding additional organizational funding to keep up with the backlog of customer requested enhancements. Based on conversations with Retire Inc. leaders, Mai realized it would be difficult to secure the funding required to build an effective centralized function at this time. Additionally, the time to hire new staff, effectively onboard them, and then start to standardize data management practices would take too long before the centralized analytics function would be able to provide data to other departments.

Mai felt decentralizing the analytics function with the current lack of data maturity was risky and could result in poor use of data, corrupted data, data silos being created throughout Retire Inc, or proliferation of unsecured sensitive data. This could lead to poor decisions, stalled progress, or worse yet, irresponsible use of customer data. She assessed the risk to be high and it would set back the organization for many years - she could not recommend a fully decentralized structure.

The final deciding point for the recommendation was the fact that although the RetireSafe backlog was long, it would reduce significantly over time. She estimated that the current team was sufficient to manage this workload and reasoned that over time, there would be less and less requests for additional enhancements.

.6 Key Takeaways

- It often takes one successful analytics driven project to open the floodgates for data requests. Organizations often transition between centralized, decentralized, and hybrid models as needs dictate and data maturity evolves.
- Recommendations do not have to be an "either-or" decision. In this case, a hybrid recommendation of initially allowing the RetireSafe product team to make foundational data management decisions could prove to be the most cost-effective way to build organizational-level data management strategies. Transitioning to a centralized data management function in the future would then allow much broader use of data in a disciplined, organized, and secure way throughout Retire Inc.
- Decisions often go far beyond the "pros and cons" analysis as many other factors come into play.
- How best to structure the business data analytics function at an organizational level can be a complex challenge and context is everything.
- Important considerations including analytics maturity, existing workload, available budget, and political considerations help drive decisions to centralize, decentralize or a hybrid approach to building organizational level data capability.

3 Techniques

3.1 Business Simulation

3.1.1 Purpose

Business Simulation is a set of techniques used to model an outcome or a real-world scenario where the degree of uncertainty is high. Simulation produces reasonably good decision aids for stakeholders where outcomes dynamically change within the given context.

3.1.2 Description

Business Simulation uses a model-first approach where a representative model of a real-world interaction is created. The representation is based on domain experience, expert knowledge, knowledge of business processes, and by observing how actors interact and make decisions in that environment. Data can be fed into the model and the results of the simulation can be used to identify or predict optimal actions.

The following characteristics describe an effective business simulation:

- Uses many business hypotheses to create a model of the real-world process or the environment.
- Requires extensive analysis to derive the root causes for some business actions.
- May use real-time information versus historical data to prescribe actions.
- Models hard to predict outcomes with many influencing causes. The outcomes can be demonstrated through simulation tools.

Business simulation is used in the following types of scenarios:

- Where data is sparse. For example, for a new software product launch.
- Where intangible variables are involved. For example, modelling the of goodwill on product sales, social experience, or brand value.
- Where what-if scenarios and business test cases are involved. For example, what happens to customer adoption of a product if the price is increased by 10%?
- When live experimentation is not possible or feasible. For example, the impact of a merger between two organizations.

3.1.3 Elements

.1 Scale and Scope of Business Simulation

The scale and scope of the simulation involves determining the business scenarios and extent of the simulation that needs to be attempted. For example, simulation can be used for complete business operations, specific market and economic changes, or it can be applied to support simple business decisions. The scale of the simulation determines the extent of analysis required for building the model.

Depending on the business scenario, the following types of simulations can be attempted:

- ***Risk simulation***: Use a multitude of factors to simulate outcomes when large scale changes are made to the business process or economic conditions. For example, market crashes, sovereign risks, or business risks such as mergers and acquisitions.
- ***Event-based simulation***: It is sometimes difficult to anticipate what changes will occur if some variables are changed. The prominent examples are what-if and sensitivity analysis where a new event is injected into the model and the results are studied.
- ***Dynamic simulation***: Involves modelling both actions and reactions in a dynamic business environment.

The following demonstrates the interaction between the simulation model and the analysts who create the simulation model based on expert knowledge.

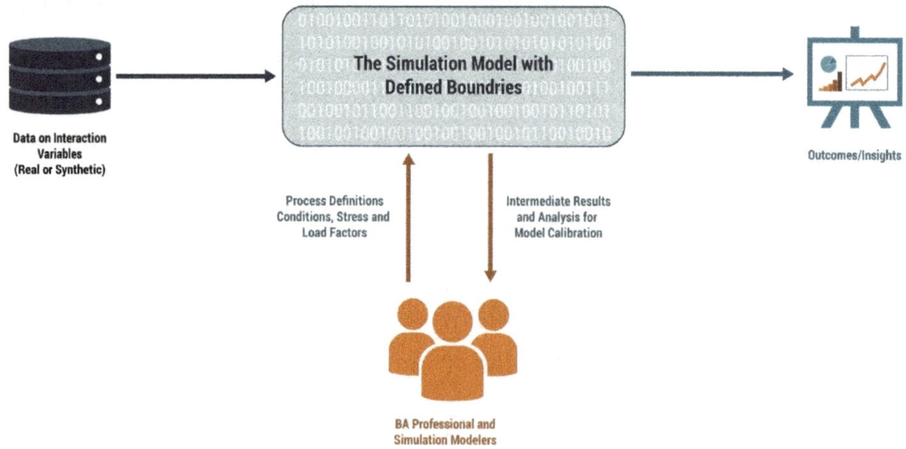

.2 Variables and their Distribution

For a simulation experiment, input variables play a critical role. Analysts determine what variables influence the outcome, based on their experience and knowledge of the real-world scenario being modelled,

A simulation model can be used when there isn't enough real-world data available. A simulation model can use synthetic data or use perceived distribution of the data. Often missing data can be modelled through distributions.

.3 Domain Knowledge, Processes, and Business Constraints

Business rules, systems knowledge, and events are key information that analysts uncover using other techniques. These are then modelled mathematically or heuristically to pre-configure the simulation model. Complex interactions between input variables are then modelled using the process and business knowledge embedded into the simulation model.

.4 Model Outcome and Orchestration

When a business scenario is simulated, outcomes can be measured and demonstrated. Unlike other predictive analytics approaches, simulation can handle different business scenario inputs and present the changed outcome. Analysts then identify and interpret the outcomes of simulations for key stakeholders. These models are often self-contained and produce visual results that business stakeholders could use via a self-service mode by providing different business test cases (for example, by changing the input variable values) to see the effect.

3.1.4 Usage Considerations

.1 Strengths

- Cause-action-reaction chains can be modelled without disrupting the business.
- Complex business situations can be modelled with accurate inputs.
- Simulations are computationally efficient and involve lower data acquisition cost.
- They are accurate for business scenarios with many contributing factors and a low amount of data.
- Simulations can be used in modelling prescriptive actions and predictions under business constraints.

.2 Limitations

- Creating effective simulations requires expert knowledge of the system being simulated.
- The outcome of a simulation experiment can be difficult to explain due to the many variables involved.
- Other types of modelling techniques are considered more effective (for example, reinforcement learning), and neural networks are becoming more accurate in driving simulation outcomes.

3.2 Business Visualizations

3.2.1 Purpose

Business visualizations are used to communicate insights drawn from data with business stakeholders. They differ from technical visualizations which are aids for the analytics professionals to draw and understand insights from data.

3.2.2 Description

Business visualizations are used in most types of analytics initiatives. For example, in a descriptive analytics initiative where stakeholders want to understand the health of their business, outcomes expressed as visualizations typically include dashboards and reports. Visuals are also used to convey many of the relevant facts from data that may have a bearing on the business or research problem. Analysts may also choose business visuals to communicate exploratory data analysis (EDA) results, conclusions, or the analytics process.

Unlike technical visuals which have well-defined forms, business visuals are fit for purpose and developed specifically to communicate key insights. Many visuals are interactive, combining data and information, conclusions, or data journeys that describe the data analysis process. Business analysis professionals work closely with information designers and user experience personnel to generate effective business visualizations.

Some guidelines for creating business visuals include:

- ***Know the research problem and the insight being communicated***: The business context and the resulting outcomes of analysis direct the choice of the business visual. If a graph is selected, but unsuited for the research problem or doesn't convey the insight clearly, then that choice of visualization would fail to achieve the desired result.

  For example, a research problem involves the study of sales across different regions. Upon analysis, the insight identifies a certain region over-performing compared to the previous year, but under-performing in the current year compared to other regions. Although the first data set may seem more appealing as a visual, the second data set depicts both the year-over-year (YOY) performance comparison for each region and the performance comparison between regions.

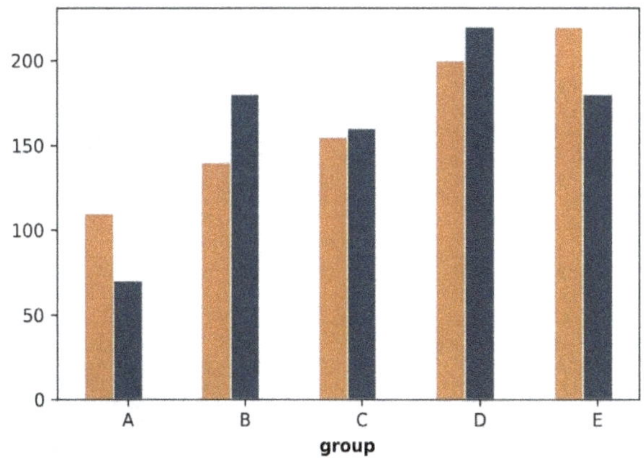

- ***Know your stakeholders***: Knowledge about business stakeholders such as their interest areas, motivation, technical acumen, and availability, helps analyst determine the level of information to present. Analysts work with key stakeholders to identify the level of detail required and then determine what type of visual best meets that need.

  For example, a stakeholder may want to understand a holistic metric; overall budget spend versus budget allocated. If there is no need to track the daily budget spend versus budget allocated, then representation of the aggregate metric through a percentage visual is more appropriate (similar to the second visual).

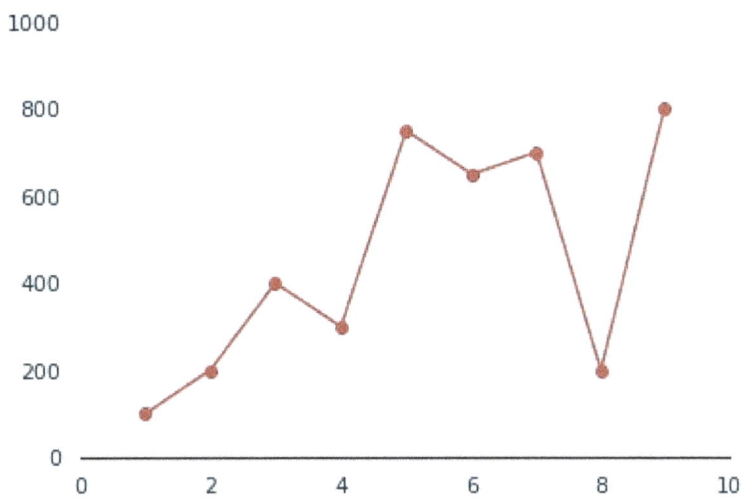

- ***Present unbiased analysis***: Data can be inadvertently presented in a favourable light, to confirm the opinions of key stakeholders, or provide one's own opinion on what the representation may mean. The purpose of a business visual is to help stakeholders "see" the insight rather than direct stakeholders to a biased opinion.

  For example, the graphs below show a simple example where the scale of the Y-axis is different although both graphs are presenting the same data. The audience may have a biased opinion if the first image is presented.

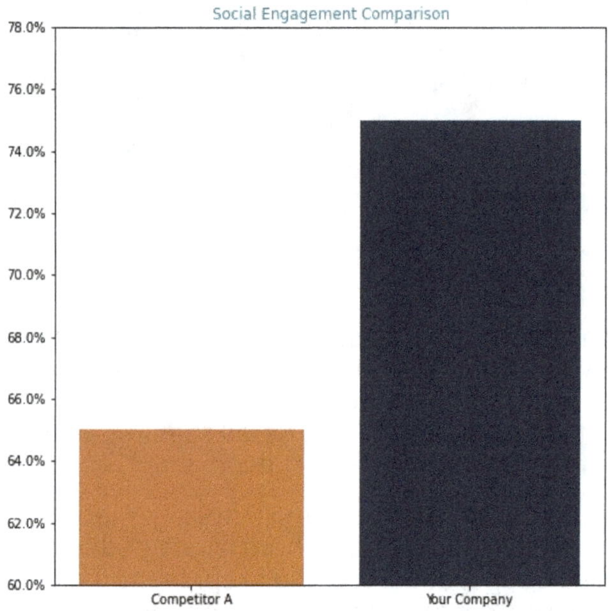

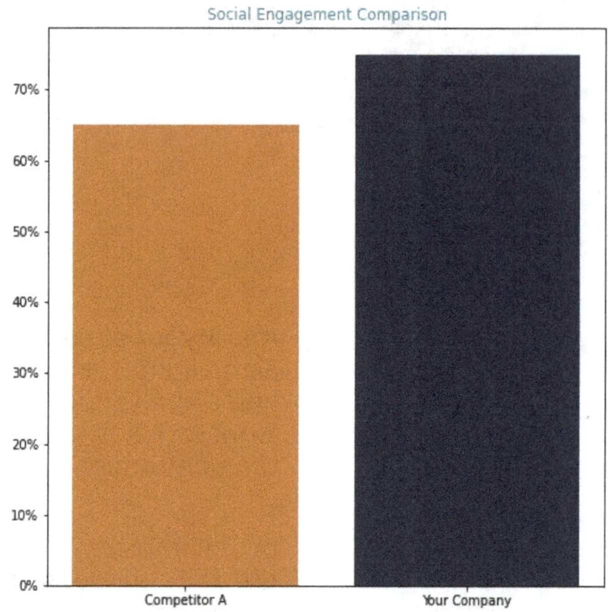

- ***Avoid complexity - function over form***: With the advances in visualization tools and technologies, it is possible to produce visuals that are increasingly complex. However, simpler graphics are easier to understand and powerfully capture the insight. A visual which is highly appealing may not be the best option if a simpler alternative is available. Less context and instructions are needed to interpret a simpler graphic. Analysts should focus on the message rather than the aesthetics of a visual.

For example, both diagrams below introduce a third dimension to the data. It may be difficult to interpret the relative coordinates of the data points in the first image, whereas the second image can provide a clearer sense of the third dimension with the size of the data points.

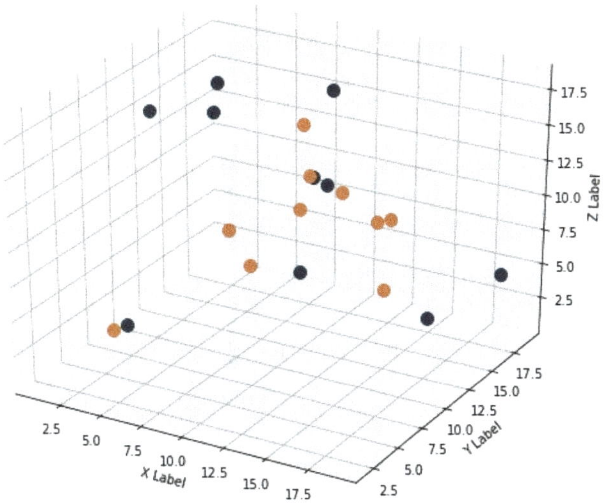

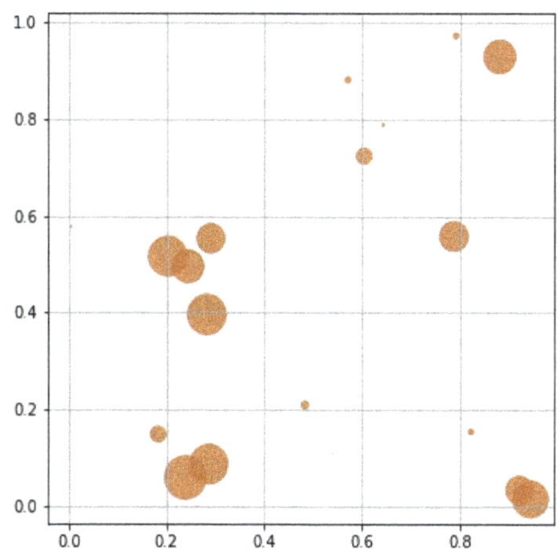

- ***Stand out from the rest***: When all other considerations such as the intent, the level of detail, and stakeholder preferences are equal between two visuals, it is advisable to have a visual stand out. Stakeholders can get fatigued by looking at similar visuals. Although the insight may be useful. the message may get lost and this risk can be minimized by using a more unique visualization.

The competencies required to create visualizations are shared between analysts, data science professionals, and user experience designers. It is helpful to collaborate with other practitioners to develop business visualizations that create a lasting impact.

3.2.3 Elements

.1 Purpose and Types of Visuals

The purpose of the visual plays a critical role in communicating the message and the selection of the type of visual must suit this purpose.

Two questions can be used to understand the purpose of the visuals:

- is the visual to be declarative or exploratory, and
- is the information in the visual going to be conceptual or data-driven?

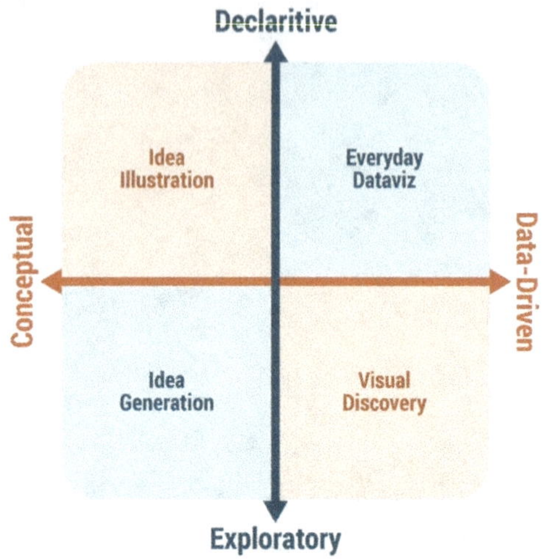

Answering these two questions positions the decision in one of four quadrants. Based on the quadrant the visual might have different purposes, which helps in deciding the right graph, chart, or diagram.

- ***Idea illustration***: requires decomposing complex ideas into simple, clear visuals that rely on the ability to understand metaphors and analogies. Gartner's Hype Cycle is a good example of this type of visual. Process models, infographics, and framework visuals are other examples that take a large amount of data and illustrate the idea in an intuitive way.
- ***Idea generation:*** helps during the discovery process. They include mental models, mind maps, conceptual metaphors, or simple objects that help you evolve your thinking.
- ***Everyday dataviz***: are routinely used by business people and include bar charts and pie charts. The key is to simplify and focus on communicating single messages through each visual.
- ***Visual discovery***: are the most complicated. They are primarily used to discover new insights and for visual confirmation of business hypotheses. Both data and exploration may require significant adjustments to different chart types to fit the purpose.

Everyday dataviz are simple visuals used for primarily for story telling and context setting.

.2 Types of Data

Selecting an appropriate visual depends on the type of data and the limitations that are associated with that data type. The type of data available and the way the data is required to be presented determines which types of visualizations are more suitable. The data may be used to present the following:

- ***Comparison***: Compare two or more categories over time or by items or amounts. Bar charts, line charts, butterfly charts, among others are ideal.
- ***Composition***: Show a whole that is composed of different items, for example, sales by different product lines or line of business. Stacked bar charts, waterfalls, and area charts are all good options.
- ***Distribution***: Show distributions of different data elements or predictors. Line charts, histograms, and scatter plots are useful.
- ***Relationships***: Illustrate relationships between data elements. Scatter plots, heat maps, chords, and venn diagrams can be used.

.3 Key Message and Supplementary Texts

The visual is not always enough for stakeholders to "see" trends and patterns or draw insights. The context of the visual, the data element, key statistics, and legends are also explained. The story or the narrative establishes the context, whereas the key messages can be embedded into visuals without crowding the visuals.

3.2.4 Usage Considerations

.1 Strengths

- Business visualization is a powerful tool when combined with storytelling.
- Business visuals are much more effective in facilitating discussions and helping business stakeholders understand data insights.
- Business visuals can be used in various contexts which make them a versatile tool for interpreting and reporting results of analytics initiatives.
- Most stakeholders are familiar with using visuals to understand large amounts of data, so business visualizations can have a big impact with decision-makers.

.2 Limitations

- Business visualization may direct stakeholders to believe an incorrect conclusion that was a result of biased representation of the data.
- Visualizations require processing a large amount of data and are prone to data errors.
- Business visuals are mostly summaries, minor but relevant trends or facts may get overlooked.
- Data visualization requires strong storytelling and data orchestration skills which limits the use of standalone visuals.

3.3 Concept Modelling

3.3.1 Purpose

A concept model is used to organize the business vocabulary needed to communicate the knowledge of a domain consistently and thoroughly.

For more information, see *A Guide to the Business Analysis Body of Knowledge (BABOK® Guide)* v3, chapter 10.11.

3.3.2 Business Data Analytics Perspective

In data analytics initiatives, concept models are used to describe a data solution from a business perspective including business context, business terms, and key concepts. They help determine scope and help identify interrelationships between the various components. Concept models are also useful as reference materials when identifying or planning for data sources and during data analysis to provide the business context to the data.

.1 Identify the Research Question

Concept models are typically created early in a data analytics initiative, when identifying the research question. They provide the analytics team with a way to represent the future state, described from a business perspective.

Key characteristics of concept models include:

- capturing key business entities such as:
  - concepts,
  - persons or roles,
  - events, and
  - places and any other business-specific items for which data needs to be captured.
- establishing the use of relevant business terms, rules, and concepts.
- containing both visuals and text to explain the model.
- accommodating future changes and expansions.

During identification of research questions, concept models help:

- describe use or application of key business terms, rules, and functionality, as well as interrelationships between business components,
- provide an initial, high-level assessment of data required for tracking,
- communicate and validate business scope with stakeholders,
- evaluate and modify existing research questions, as needed,
- act as a base model for other more technical, logical, and physical models,

- establish a strong starting point for requirements analysis and design, and
- serve as a reference document that can be revisited for future purposes (for example, when a solution needs to undergo complex changes).

.2 Source Data

Concept models are a useful resource when identifying either existing data sources or opportunities for new data sources. They also establish the relationships that exist between various data points.

.3 Analyze Data

Concept models provide the business view to the data and its relationships. They also act as base models when building on the logical and physical models.

.4 Interpret and Report Results

Concept Modelling does not have a significant role in the Interpret and Report Results domain. However, it can be used to illustrate complex business vocabulary that is part of the outcomes the team wishes to share with the rest of the organization.

.5 Use Results to Influence Business Decision-Making

Concept Modelling does not have a significant role in Use Results to Influence Business Decision-Makings domain. However, it can be used to visually simplify complex outcomes from the analytics effort.

.6 Guide Organization-Level Strategy for Business Analytics

Concept Modelling does not have a significant role in the Guide Organization-Level Strategy for Business Analytics domain. However, it can be used to illustrate or describe important information about the business analytics function.

3.4 Data Dictionary

3.4.1 Purpose

A data dictionary is used to standardize a definition of a data element and enable a common interpretation of data elements within a single data source or across multiple data sources.

For more information, see *BABOK® Guide* v3, chapter 10.12.

3.4.2 Business Data Analytics Perspective

The data dictionary is used to collate and standardize references to data elements across initiatives or at an organizational level. In a business data analytics initiative, the data dictionary can also be expanded to identify and locate data elements across organizational systems. To achieve this, the primitive elements in a data dictionary including name, aliases, value or meaning, and description can be expanded to also track business rules and data validation, both for derived data and transformed elements.

A comprehensive data dictionary serves as a source of truth for the team in determining the business data analytics approach and subsequent tasks.

.1 Identify the Research Question

When planning the business data analytics approach, it is important to determine what relevant data currently exists. The data dictionary is used to understand and select key data elements, either to frame good quality questions or to identify data to be explored through the questions. The data dictionary provides all stakeholders with a shared understanding of data elements, their use, and their application.

.2 Source Data

When sourcing data, the data dictionary helps to identify the required data sources, study key data elements, and perform data mapping, migrations, and transformations. For example, queries used to source data may use data elements as conditional filters, and their data type, format, and size are essential to understand. The data dictionary provides a deeper understanding of data elements and how they may be related to other data elements, and this helps identify a comprehensive set of data sources.

.3 Analyze Data

The data dictionary can be used in conjunction with other models, such as entity relationship diagrams, to understand how to join data between different data sources and perform the necessary analysis.

.4 Interpret and Report Results

Data Dictionary does not have a significant role in the Interpret and Report Results domain. However, important outcomes of the analytics effort may result in new elements being defined and these can be added to the data dictionary.

.5 Use Results to Influence Business Decision-Making

Data Dictionary does not have a significant role in the Use Results to Influence Business Decision-Making domain. However, the team may reference the existing data dictionary to ensure results are being communicated in a standardized and meaningful way.

.6 Guide Organization-Level Strategy for Business Analytics

Data Dictionary does not have a significant role in the Guide Organization-Level Strategy for Business Analytics domain. However, the analytics team can refer to the data dictionary and help maintain its relevance as new terms are developed.

3.5 Data Flow Diagrams

3.5.1 Purpose

Data flow diagrams show where data comes from, which activities process the data, and if the output results are stored or utilized by another activity or external entity.

For more information, see *BABOK® Guide* v3, chapter 10.13.

3.5.2 Business Data Analytics Perspective

Data flow diagrams illustrate the movement and transformation of data between entities and processes. They are used to depict and identify data that is relevant to the business data analytics initiative.

.1 Identify the Research Question

Various types of data flow diagrams are used to understand organizational data. Logical data flow diagrams are used to assess the current state of data and help depict the future state. Physical data flow diagrams identify data sources involved and how data flows between them. This knowledge helps the data analytics team frame better quality research questions.

.2 Source Data

When sourcing data, data flow diagrams are beneficial in identifying the required data sources, the data dependencies, and the best ways to bring together the data into the target repository.

.3 Analyze Data

Data flow diagrams are beneficial during data analysis, particularly when trying to identify the source of any data discrepancies. Data issues can be introduced during data migration or transformation, or even due to incorrect data mapping. These models are used to understand data anomalies and help the team identify how best to improve data quality.

.4 Interpret and Report Results

Data Flow Diagrams does not have a significant role in the Interpret and Report Results domain. However, it can be used to support the narrative being constructed.

.5 Use Results to Influence Business Decision-Making

The results of the data analytics work can be depicted or illustrated using data flow diagrams, where appropriate. They aid understanding by visualizing data flows that may be difficult to understand. For example, future state physical data flow diagrams help implement any new data sources or data processes required for the future state.

.6 Guide Organization-Level Strategy for Business Analytics

Although Data Flow Diagrams is not specifically used to guide organization-level strategy, they are used to describe the flow of data across processes that are used by the data analytics team.

3.6 Data Mapping

.1 Purpose

Data mapping is used to consolidate data from one or more sources to a destination to create a meaningful set of data with a standardized format. This ensures that data can be accessed and used for business reporting and analysis.

.2 Description

Organizations collect a lot of data from many different data points, stored in varied formats. During data sourcing, there is often a need to migrate one or more of these data sources into a single data repository where all data has a consistent format. This allows for easy access to the data and reporting across the organization. Data mapping establishes a relationship between the source and the target repository, allowing data migration to happen, despite potentially disparate data formats.

Data mapping is used to support:

- data migration, where source data is moved to a new data repository, and
- data integration, where source data is merged with an existing data repository.

  Note: For data integration to be possible, at a minimum, the data models of both source and target should be the same, even if the data schemas are different.

Data mapping happens at the attribute-level. During data migration and integration, attention is given to:

- the selected attributes that will be migrated from source to target.
- creation of new attributes in the target repository to allow migration from the source.
- data type and size of the target attribute that is defined to ensure it can accommodate the source attribute data. In some instances, it may be determined the data size of the target attribute should be the same as the source data size, while in other instances the data size for the target attribute may need to be larger so it can accommodate future expansion. However, the target data size should never be smaller than the source data size as that may result in missing data.
- new custom-defined attributes that involve some form of manipulation or calculation (for example, tax amount, product name based on product code).

Data integration also requires the analysis of the common attributes between source and target repositories and the nature of their relationship (for example, one-to-one and zero-to-many).

The complexity of data mapping may depend on several factors including the degree of disparity between the source and target repositories, and any existing data hierarchy.

3.6.1 Elements

.1 Source

The repository providing the original data is referred to as the source. When analyzing the source, analysts consider the:

- format of the source (for example, delimited file, spreadsheet, database entity),
- attributes of interest or potential interest, and
- data type and data size of the attributes.

.2 Target

The repository receiving the data is referred to as the target. When analyzing the target, analysts consider the:

- format of the source (for example, delimited file, spreadsheet, database entity),
- new attributes that need to be created within the target to align with the source, with similar data type and data sizes,
- source attributes that need to be transformed in the target and their corresponding transformation rule. These could be based on a business rule or a business requirement (for example, the "TransactionDatetime" data attribute in the source has a datetime format of mm/dd/yyyy hh:mm:tt but in the target only the date should be brought in for easy querying purposes. So, the TransactionDate attribute in the target will have the date format mm/dd/yyyy), and
- creation of new custom fields (for example, adding a calculation, combining attributes, or formatting content based on a logic).

.3 Data Mapping Specification

Data mapping is often completed using a spreadsheet where target attributes are mapped to source attributes with applicable transformation logic. The following is a basic data map.

Target			Source	Transformation Rules	
Entity Name	**Attribute Name**	**Data Type**	**Attribute(s)**	**Direct Map?**	**Logic**
T_Employee	Emp_ID	Varchar (10)	Employee.ID	Y	
T_Employee	Emp_Name	Varchar (50)	Employee.FirstName, Employee.LastName	N	Concatenate (Employee.FirstName, " ", EmployeeLastName)
T_Employee	Emp_DepNo	Number (2)	Employee.Departnment Number	Y	
T_Employee	Emp_StartDate	Date	Employee.StartDate	Y	Only bring the date component with format YYYY-MM-DD

3.6.2 Usage Considerations

.1 Strengths

- Provides a meticulous approach to ensuring smooth migration and integration of data between varied data platforms.
- Provides data traceability, which is particularly beneficial when resolving data issues.
- Easy to learn and use.
- Enables creation of a standardized, business-focused data repository, which in turn allows for consistency and ease in data access and reporting.
- Helps identify any data quality issues within the source or the target.

.2 Limitations

- Requires careful attention to detail to avoid encountering data loss, redundancies, or other unexpected errors.
- Data mapping work, particularly when done manually, can be time-consuming.
- Needs updating as soon as changes are made in either source or target.

3.7 Data Storytelling

3.7.1 Purpose

Data storytelling is used to communicate data in a meaningful way. An engaging narrative provides business context and highlights key insights to drive better business decisions.

3.7.2 Description

Numbers, graphs, and charts have little meaning without business context. Combining data, visuals, and a narrative has a more impactful influence on decision-making. This is where data storytelling comes in.

Data storytelling is a structured way to communicate and ensure engagement from both an analytical and emotional perspective. It helps provide an engaging and insightful experience of sharing data results with key stakeholders in the Interpret and Report Results domain.

While data visuals and insights are central to data presentations, the story narrative makes data storytelling influential and effective. It considerably increases the odds of the right decision being made at the right time.

To enable clear, robust, and visually appealing communication, data stories follow these key principles:

- ***Understand the audience***: Stakeholder analysis informs how the insight is communicated, what level of detail is included, and how it is represented.
- ***Provide the context***: A strong narrative does two things: it provides business context by associating insights with business events, and it draws out the key insights from visuals. The more invested stakeholders are in the business context, the more impactful the narrative becomes.
- ***Use space and visuals effectively***: The medium to create the visuals is selected to display the visuals in their best light. The right visuals to easily and effectively share the key insights are selected. Consideration is given to the size of the text and visuals, their orientation, and the colours used.
- ***Communicate as a story***: Effective visuals, supported by context and key focus points, are shared in a story format: an introduction, a middle where the plot develops with twists and turns, and the end that includes lessons learned and other key insights.
- ***Focus attention on key highlights***: In the Analyze Data domain, a lot of data is analyzed to draw key conclusions. Primary and secondary data insights are differentiated, and the focus is on the primary insights. Primary insights are those that directly answer the research questions. Secondary insights provide supporting context or rationale. Secondary insights may be included in the narrative, but not included in the dashboard or report.
- ***Be concise and avoid cluttering***: Particular attention is given to each element added to the page or screen. Anything that is not adding value is removed. Reviewing the content helps to ensure that key highlights and

takeaways are not lost an overly wordy narrative. The messaging should be simple and succinct, yet impactful.

3.7.3 Elements

.1 Audience

It is important to understand who the audience is, what questions they want answered, questions they may ask, as well as what they need to know.

When analyzing the audience, consider:

- the level of detail to include,
- how the results will be communicated (for example, formality, tone, use of technical language), and
- the relationship with the audience (for example, a trusted expert will include next steps while a novice analyst may recommend actions).

.2 Narrative

By keeping data dashboards and presentations succinct, a lot of content from the analysis is not shown. The narrative includes the information that is not included but is important to the story. It also provides the rationale for the dips and spikes in the charts by correlating to specific incidents or events. Narrative explains the visual and provides context to key insights.

.3 Visualization

To make it easy to discern the meaning of the data, it is important to leverage the appropriate visualization, and use colours and formatting strategically to provide visual cues to the key insights or conclusions.

When creating a visualization, analysts consider:

- the appropriate visualization to use,
- the colours and the manner in which colour contrasting is leveraged,
- size of visuals and text, based on importance, and other text formatting (for example, bold, italics, underline), and
- positioning and order of items on the page or screen.

These design considerations help ensure that the most important insights are easy and quick to discern.

.4 Storytelling

While validated insights may be sufficient to make decisions, the emotional aspect of decision-making is often lacking. Emotions are essential to decision-making. Storytelling aids in bringing out the emotional aspect of perceiving information.

Data storytelling follows the same structure as a story. The introduction sets up the context and introduces key elements, the middle builds on the plot with a focus on wins and challenges, and it concludes with key insights and lessons learned. This format makes the experience more appealing and stimulating. A well-engaged and educated audience, in turn, makes better decisions.

Analysts consider the following principles for influential data storytelling:

- keep the language simple,
- any sentence or part of the narrative that is not contributing value should be eliminated,
- the order of the narrative (spoken and written) should make sense (a disorderly story can lose the audience's attention),
- ensure the purpose of each visual is clear, and
- summarize key points in the conclusion.

3.7.4 Usage Considerations

.1 Strengths

- Provides a holistic comprehension of the results.
- Engages the audience emotionally and activates more parts of the brain when compared to solely fact-based presentations.
- Enables the audience to focus on the key insights and takeaways and what they means in the business context.
- A compelling narrative will influence and drive better decisions.

.2 Limitations

- Crafting a story around the data can be time-consuming.
- Creative story writing is an art and can be harder to write than the traditional messaging around data reporting. The effectiveness of the narrative is dependent on the writer's skills.
- If bias and self-motivated interests drive the storytelling and only data that support their case are shared, then the audience will be misled.

3.8 Decision Modelling and Analysis

3.8.1 Purpose

Decision modelling shows how repeatable business decisions are made.

For more information, see *BABOK® Guide* v3, chapter 10.17.

Decision analysis formally assesses a problem and possible decisions in order to determine the value of alternate outcomes under conditions of uncertainty.

For more information, see *BABOK® Guide v3*, chapter 10.16.

3.8.2 Business Data Analytics Perspective

Decision modelling helps demonstrate how data and knowledge are combined to make decisions, and decision analysis is used to examine the possible consequences of different decisions about a given problem. Both techniques are used extensively in business data analytics. Benefits of using decision modelling and analysis in business data analytics initiatives include:

- assessing the business decisions that need research and verifying if they align with the overall business strategy of the organization.
- verifying whether the research questions stem from the right business objectives the organization wants to assess.
- studying and modelling organizational decision-making and the architecture established so that repeatable decisions can be made.
- identifying root causes and appropriate actions based on understanding the business decision-making framework in an organization.
- analyzing complex organizational challenges by using advanced decision analysis models such as multi-criteria decision making (MCDM), game design, goal programming, simulations, and case base reasoning.

.1 Identifying the Research Question

Organizations rarely make decisions in isolation, and many decisions are part of the enterprise architecture model that drives a sequence of decisions or consequences. Identifying and analyzing potential impact of specific decisions can lead to forming higher-quality research questions. Decision modelling and analysis activities include:

- discovering decisions that require an analytical inference and entities affected by such decisions,
- prioritizing decisions that would most contribute to the business objective,
- enumerating decision alternatives in MCDM and similar approaches, and
- identifying the appropriate research question for each of these alternatives.

The necessary analysis tends to be more complex than decision trees, tables, or empirical cause and analysis. Selecting the appropriate decision modelling technique and the most effective decision analysis approach plays an important role in forming higher quality research questions.

.2 Source Data

Decision Modelling and Analysis do not have a significant role in the Source Data domain. However, the outcomes of decision analysis can help identify or validate source data.

.3 Analyze Data

Decision Modelling and Analysis do not have a significant role in the Analyze Data domain. However, the outcomes of decision analysis can support the overall data analysis work.

.4 Interpret and Report Results

Decision Modelling and Analysis do not have a significant role in the Interpret and Report Results domain. However, the results being reported may impact future decision models and decision analysis frameworks being used in the organization.

.5 Use Results to Influence Business Decision-Making

Decision Modelling and Analysis plays a significant role, after studying the analytics result, in the team's assessment and recommendations. The baseline decision model established during the identification of the research question phase is utilized to assess how analytical insights affect business decisions. Decision Modelling and Analysis can be used to influence business decisions by:

- evaluating conflicting insights and outcomes through the decision analysis process (for example, a decision tree can be used to follow a business decision to its logical impact).
- prioritizing business decisions that are most aligned to the organization's strategy.
- formulating relevant recommendations based on understanding the impact of business decisions and their dependencies.
- allowing decisions to be integrated with the relevant business processes by an assessment of benefits.

.6 Guide Organization-Level Strategy for Business Analytics

Decision Modelling and Analysis do not have a significant role in the Guide Organization-Level Strategy for Business Analytics domain. However, Decision Modelling and Analysis are used to address challenges determining the optimal organizational level practices for business analytics.

3.9 Descriptive and Inferential Statistics

3.9.1 Purpose

Descriptive statistics derive information about the population under study. Inferential statistics helps to assess information about a sample of the population and make informed generalizations. Together, they are important techniques through which business information is quantified, compared, or predicted.

3.9.2 Description

Business data is generally plentiful in most organizations. The challenge is how to interpret and use that data. The first step is to quantify the data in meaningful ways so it can be compared, contrasted, and assessed to discern trends. Once quantified, the data needs to be interpreted in the context of the business to drive important insights. These insights can then be used to support business decision-making. Descriptive and inferential statistics provide powerful tools and techniques for addressing these challenges.

Descriptive statistics are a set of formal techniques and tools that allow summarization of data and provide the means to describe that data. Most of these tools are rooted in reality and how people naturally understand data. For example, if an organization's sales figures need to be compared across quarters, the most natural way to think about it is the average sales.

Inferential statistics provide the tools and methods to infer some meaning from statistical summaries that are based on a sample size representation of the overall population that is under study. Most analytical methods are based on this and extensions of these concepts. For example, most advanced analytics, machine learning applications, and neural nets use inferential statistics methods as their first principle.

An introduction to descriptive statistics and inferential statistics is presented in this technique. This technique purposely avoids the mathematical complexity inherent in these approaches. Statistical textbooks can be referenced for more detailed explanations, as needed.

3.9.3 Elements

.1 Descriptive Statistics

The foundational concepts of descriptive statistics include:

- ***Types of data***: There are different types of data used in an analytics exercise in its most atomic form. Revenue, sales, profit, and age are continuous data. The number of employees, number of items ordered, and number of stocks purchased are discrete-valued data. Data that represent different types of categories such as gender, types of products of a company, and different departments are categorical data. If there is an order to the categorical data then it is referred to as ordinal data, such as grades in a subject (for example, A, B, C).

Mixing up types of data in data sourcing is not helpful for analysis. For example, treating ordinal data as categorical will not provide accurate analysis as the order is ignored; that is, a grade A and grade F in a subject are treated equally in the analysis.

- ***Organization of data***: Most business data is either structured or unstructured. Structured data, often referred to as rectangular data, are highly organized. The relation between each element is pre-defined and managed through rules. Unstructured data, on the other hand, are an aggregation of non-homogenous types of data.

  Depending on the analytics context, structured and unstructured data can be used. For faster access, processing, and computation, structured data can be used. If volume and variety of data is needed, unstructured data may work better.

- ***Measures of central tendency/location***: This is the most natural way to summarize data by saying where the data is most concentrated. Mean (average) is the sum of values over the number of items. Median is the value that halves the data (50% on either side of the median value). Mode represents the most frequent value observed in the data. Quantiles and percentiles are the values that partition the data into several pieces.

  The use of a measure is contextual to the research problem. Mean is susceptible to outliers, the median is not used universally, and mode values can be many within a dataset. Median is often used as a data imputation value when the data is missing.

- ***Measures of deviation***: Mean values alone may not describe the data fully. For example, consider two stocks with the same yearly mean return but one of the stock's daily returns fluctuates wildly. This indicates the other stock is most likely less risky to purchase. This concept leads to measuring the variation in data captured through variance and standard deviation that can be used to describe how much the data is dispersed around the mean.

  Variance is the square of standard deviation and not in the same unit as mean. It may prove confusing for business stakeholders to interpret this type of data. However, variance is a common measure used in analytics models. Skewness and kurtosis are higher-order measures that describe the shape of the distribution of values around the mean.

- ***Sample measures***: It is often difficult to measure the entirety of the population; using a sample set can be sufficient. For example, it is not advisable to survey every customer of a company to identify quality issues with service delivery. All the measures described such as mean and variance apply to sample sets and can be used to estimate the population parameters.

  The sample statistics only estimate the population parameter. There are small differences in the way parameters are estimated for the moments around the mean (for example, variance, skewness, et al). The values are adjusted to reflect accurate values when used in modelling or for reporting purposes.

- ***Probability basics***: Probability is a branch of mathematics and statistics that is heavily used for analytical modelling. All outcomes and predictions are not certain events but only likely events. The probability of some event is computed as the expected outcome over the possible outcomes. The expected value is calculated as a weighted mean of values with associated probabilities. For example, if an insurer wants to predict the expected claim value for an automobile and the insurer expects the claims to be either $2,000, vehicle damage, $1.500 collision and $1000 for liability with probabilities 0.5, 0.3 and 0, then the expected claim amount is 2x0.5+1.5x.3+0.2x1=$1.65000.

  Most predictive problems use probabilities and expected value as outputs. It is possible to optimize the wrong measure in an analytics problem. For example, an organization targeting a lower rate of attrition may be optimizing probability of employees leaving, but it should focus on the expected value of the loss of business due to attrition.

- ***Multivariate measures***: When summarizing more than one variable, the focus of analysis is on understanding their interrelationships. For example, the total sale may depend on advertising spend and the number of distribution channels. To establish such relationships, covariance and correlation are used. That is, for a small change in one variable, how much change is expected in the other? Correlation is a scaled version of covariance which ranges between -1 and 1. High correlation, positive or negative, in the right context suggests a relationship.

  Correlation between both dependent and independent variables needs to be studied. In the example, if the distribution channel and advertisement spend are highly correlated, there is a possibility of double counting on sales. Covariance and correlation have many applications in modelling. For example, dimensionality reduction of data which helps simplify the analysis.

- ***Probability distributions***: Distribution of a variable refers to the probability of encountering different values around the mean value. For example, daily sales numbers and their associated probabilities in a year, if plotted, would look like a probability distribution graph.

  Probability distribution provides a lot of information about how a variable behaves. Knowledge of various distribution types is an essential element of analytical models. The distribution graphs are best represented as visuals as they may be used for explaining the behaviour of different variables.

Statistical Tests

z -test is used to verify whether a population parameter is significantly different from some hypothesized value.

t -test is used when the number of observed values are less

f- test is used to compare population variances to sample variances.

chi square test is used to verify how well a distribution resembles a hypothesized distribution.

.2 Inferential Statistics

The foundational concepts of inferential statistics include:

- ***Statistical tests***: Statistical tests are used to conclude the summary statistics observed when describing the data. The sample statistics (for example, sample mean, variance, and so on) are used to draw inferences about the population. A z-test deduces what range an observed sample mean can take. A t-test is used instead of z-test when the number of observations in a sample is less. A chi square test is mostly used to test the variation of test statistics such as sample variances.

  Different tests apply based on the business situation. Particularly in finance and healthcare industries, these tests are industry best practices and some knowledge is expected from analysts to engage the stakeholders in an analytics context.

- ***Regression analysis***: Regression is one of the most used tools in predictive analytics. The outcome can be first related and then predicted based on one or more dependent variables. In regression analysis, the goal is to predict the values of a dependent variable based upon the values of an independent variable, so when new data is encountered, this knowledge can be applied to predict the dependent variable.

  When analysts communicate complex analytical models to business stakeholders, regression analysis can be used to explain the basic principles. However, during actual modelling activities data scientists focus on model development, and analysts support this by verifying the key factors (independent variables) using their business acumen and domain knowledge.

- ***Bayesian inference***: This is a simple model to infer population characteristics based on the application of Bayes theorem. Simply stated, this means that future values can be estimated by historical values if they can be computed from the data that exists.

  Bayesian inference is used for quick benchmarking in the industry about the success rate of predictions. It also has the added advantage that such inference can be quickly updated based on new data.

3.9.4 Usage Considerations

.1 Strengths

- Statistical methods are embedded in the core business rules of most organizations and are already used for decision-making. For analytics engagements, these concepts form the foundation for more advanced techniques.
- These concepts allow the enumeration of business decisions into quantitative values, supporting quantitative research and evidence-based decisions.
- They are a good tool to develop consensus among stakeholders as the quantitative analysis does not change.
- Most business metrics are applications of the statistical concepts and this foundational knowledge helps engage stakeholders in setting analytics goals.

.2 Limitations

- The application of statistical methods into real-world context requires many assumptions. These assumptions must be identified and recorded.
- It is not possible to identify all the factors that may influence business predictions; all predictions carry some degree of uncertainty.
- For initiatives where the influencing factors are not distinguishable, a subjective assessment may be more appropriate.
- The use of statistical methods makes the analysis more difficult to communicate without the aid of visuals and stories.

3.10 Extract, Transform, and Load (ETL)

3.10.1 Purpose

Extract, Transform, and Load (ETL) refers to a data sourcing and curation approach for application development, business intelligence, and the analytics domain. ETL is often used to make data available from a variety of sources to a target repository that acts as a single standardized source of data for further analysis to drive important insights.

3.10.2 Description

The core principles of ETL are:

- Identify high-quality data, free of data integrity and consistency errors, from a variety of sources (for example, data warehouses, data marts, data lakes, transactional databases, external websites, or mobile data).
- Transition this data to a target repository creating a "single source of truth," while applying data governance guidelines and verifying business and data rules.
- Provide easy access and the ability to use this repository of data to support analytics related work.

Big data and streaming data frequently follow different data architecture and definitions than smaller scale business data analytics initiatives. This can create a perception that ETL mechanics are irrelevant. However, the governing principles of ETL, when applied in a business data analytics context, remain the same regardless of the tools used or the approaches followed.

If applied to significantly large or diverse data, such as big data, the underlying architecture and processes to handle this data will change. For example, when using big data approaches and tools, the order of transform and load tasks may be changed or delegated to the analytics tools or solutions. Many of the tools and methods used for ETL in the context of traditional data sources use structured languages such as SQL to interact with relational databases or structured but multi-dimensional data from data warehouses.

Various architectures such as Lambda and Kappa exist for handling unstructured and distributed data. While knowledge of these architectures and distributed environments for data storage and processing is important, analysts also understand their conceptual differences, advantages, and limitations. The finer points of big data technologies, concepts, and architectures fall outside the scope of this guide.

Most analytics solutions transition through a proof of concept stage where traditional ETL processes are more relevant to analytics. Advanced big data or streaming data implementations may be used while deploying advanced analytics solutions. For example, analytics model development versus analytics model deployment. Most often, analysts conceptualize and interpret analytical solutions at the proof of concept stage.

3.10.3 Elements

.1 Extract Data

Data extraction is the first stage in the ETL process which enables identification and aggregation of data across multiple heterogeneous or homogeneous sources.

Key steps include:

1. ***Identify data sources and types***: Analysts may suggest relevant data sources and the type of data required based on the business problem to be solved. Data classifications, meta-data descriptions, and schema are usually developed through a top-down approach, starting with coarse granularity drilled down to finer granularity as the engagement progresses. For example, if the business problem involves tracking the success of a marketing campaign, the typical sources may be customer relationship management (CRM) data, sales data, and channel data. These can be drilled down to customer data, engagement data, in-store sales, online sales, marketing automation platform data, loyalty programs data, web analytics, and so on.
2. ***Create a universal classification of data***: Various data sources include different conventions and data dictionaries. When aggregating data from varied sources, the definition, description, and data formats need to be reconciled so that a uniform scheme for extraction can be used.
3. ***Verify data integrity***: Integrity of extracted data can be automatically verified during data extraction through a universal schema that maps source elements to extracted data elements (conformity of data sizes, formats, redundancy, and data transmission losses) through ETL tools. However, many of the data integrity checks can be manually performed by analysts to verify minimum values, maximum values, identifiers, valid and expected values, or by using data sampling.

.2 Transform Data

Transform Data is the translation of extracted data to a usable and accurate format. It ensures the data follows sound business logic. Analysts may be involved in verifying or prescribing the following common transformation types:

- Reconciling encoded values from the source to the target format. For example, date formats or list of values.
- Deriving calculated values. For example sales = price x units.
- Standardizing values of a variable. For example, rescaling.
- Dropping redundant attributes of an entity.
- Masking attributes. For example, social security number or credit card numbers.

- Translating text data to word vectors, specifically for Natural Language Processing (NLP) applications.
- Binning data. For example, age-to-age groups.
- Splitting strings to different columns, (for example, USIL12@# to Country|State|ID).
- Missing data imputation.
- Joins, merges, pivots, roll-ups.

Analysts play an important role in verifying that the relevant business rules are not contradicted while transforming data.

.3 Load Data

Load data involves transitioning the transformed data to a target repository (database, data warehouse, or data lake) that serves the business or analytics applications. In most cases, analytics applications interact directly with the target repository to receive and execute analytical models or generate reports based on analysis of the data. Many of the target databases involve different internal controls; some data warehouses allow only an incremental load which checks the delta between existing data and then adds changed data from the sources. This type of incremental load allows faster generation of business intelligence (BI) reports. On the other hand, a full extraction from sources may correspond to complete replacement of the data on the target system, which allows for better predictive and prescriptive analytics tasks.

The typical tasks in the load process involve:

- Reviewing target data format and load types in alignment of business need.
- Performing data load from the staging area to the target. The staging area is a logical placeholder for data which allows easy transformations.
- Generating audit trails of changed or replaced data.
- Standardizing the workflows (for example, data pipelines), which enables repeatability of the data load process. For example, when generating quarterly sales reports, once the metrics computation and data transformation requirements are finalized, there would be refreshed data available each quarter to re-generate the report.

Many of the big data technologies such as Hadoop utilize an extract, load, and then transform (ELT) sequence rather than ETL so that transformation tasks can be done at a later stage. The data storage is done through a distributed file system (for example, Hadoop Distributed File System (HDFS)), followed by data processing activities through MapReduce. This allows many big data analytics applications to use the data and experiment quickly. Analysts may provide oversight in verifying and validating whether the data loaded through such a scheme is reliable or not for business utility.

3.10.4 Usage Considerations

.1 Strengths

- Provides well-established process steps for analytics tasks primarily for descriptive analytics problems.
- Many of the ETL tools provide a graphical view of the operation and connections to enterprise data sources that facilitate easy data sourcing and self-service analytics.
- Easy maintenance of data by maintaining automatic traces to data sources and audit trails.
- Serves as a robust pre-analysis prior to modelling activities by providing a summary of the nature of the data.

.2 Limitations

- Heterogeneous and streaming data are difficult to process through traditional ETL tools and technologies.
- High-volume data movement through ETL requires a lot of planning and effort to maintain consistency.
- ETL is not suitable for near real-time interventions through algorithmic decision-making.

3.11 Exploratory Data Analysis

3.11.1 Purpose

Exploratory data analysis (EDA) is an approach used to maximize the insights gained from data by investigating, analyzing, and summarizing data to uncover relevant patterns. Exploratory data analysis often uses visual analysis to gain a comfort level with the data before applying more formal approaches such as hypothesis testing, machine learning algorithms, or advanced statistical inferences.

3.11.2 Description

EDA serves as an investigative mechanism into the problem. It is an iterative approach to understanding data where data is investigated and explored without any prior assumption or bias. Analysts use iterative discovery processes to build their understanding of the business domain and clarify the research problem.

Some of the key outcomes from EDA are:

- Recognizing the available data labels, data types, and individual characteristics of the data variables in context of the business environment and the research problem.

- Refinement of the research problem.
- Recognizing missing and incorrect data within the available data to ensure the right data is sourced for the given business problem.
- Preliminary analysis of underlying structure of the data and important data variables (features/predictors) that are relevant to the research problem.
- Understanding the interdependencies, collinearity, and correlations between data variables.
- Detecting outliers and anomalies that do not conform to the underlying data structure.
- Optimizing data variables that are most suited for more formal analysis and analytical modelling. This is often called feature engineering where derived and optimized variables are identified for further analysis.
- Preparing visual representations that communicate initial insights for different stakeholders.
- Identifying ancillary research questions or insights that may not be directly related to the research question but may be relevant to the business.

Formulations and analytical steps in a data analytics exercise depend on a technical, statistical, and mathematical background. Domain knowledge and industry knowledge also play a critical role in recognizing patterns and understanding business implications in an EDA exercise.

3.11.3 Elements

.1 Exploratory Data Analysis Scheme

Exploratory data analysis depends on investigation and exploration which allows flexibility of analysis. However, a basic step-by-step structure can be formulated to ensure common practices are followed. This foundational scheme helps analysts to take a structured approach while adapting analysis practices as needed. Activity diagrams, decision trees, and sequence diagrams all help with recording and tracking each step taken during the EDA exercise.

The following describes a typical approach:

1. Check consistency and integrity when data is loaded to the analytics platform.
    - Verify the data dimensions - number of data elements, size, data labels.
    - Verify missing data.
    - Separate training data and validation data sets.
2. Review descriptive statistics for individual variables.
    - Distribution types and shapes.

- Basic parameters - central tendencies (for example, mean, median, mode), variance, skewness, and kurtosis.

3. Verify variable inter-dependence and collinearity.
    - Correlation and variance inflation.
    - ANOVA, t-test, F-test, chi square.
4. Formulate missing data, outlier treatment, and data imputation.
    - Replacement with mean, median, mode.
    - Bayesian/algorithmic replacement.
    - Business rules application.
5. Provide appropriate visualization at relevant steps and derive preliminary insights.
6. Conduct feature engineering.
7. Build and test a basic hypothesis to test insights.
8. Refine research problems based on insights.
9. Report the initial finding with visual analysis and corroborations.

Depending on the nature of the data, different EDA schemes can be devised. For example, a data set involving images or media requires tailoring such as dimensionality reduction and vectorization as part of an EDA scheme. Similarly, natural language data may require stop words removal and part-of-speech tagging in an EDA scheme.

.2 Exploratory Data Analysis Visuals

Visuals are the primary vehicle through which the data is understood in exploratory data analysis. With visual descriptions and summarizations analysts apply pattern recognition abilities to discover insights. The right choice of visuals depends on the number of variables involved, type of data (categorical, continuous), and specific step in the EDA scheme.

Typical visualizations and graphs include:

- ***Univariate plots***: histograms, probability distribution plots, and run-sequence plots. These types of visuals show frequency or the distribution shape of a variable. For example, stock market returns for an equity are usually a negatively skewed plot when there is a higher probability of negative returns than positive returns.
- ***Bivariate plots***: bar graphs, scatter plots, boxplots, correlation plots (heat maps), and others. Bar graphs and scatter plots are good for recognizing trends, boxplots are good for identifying outliers, and correlation heat maps show interrelationship between variables.
- ***Special purpose plots***: pair plots, contour plots, and density plots all show more than two variables. For example, how does sales volume change with advertisement and delivery time? Spider charts demonstrate a dominant variable among many other variables. Lag plots, auto-correlation plots, and Box-Jenkins can all be used for time-series data. Weibull, log, and lognormal plots can all be used to visualize distributions clearly by controlling scale of axis to exponential or logarithm format.

These visualizations can be combined in many cases to provide additional insights. A careful selection of visualization, based on the need, is important.

Visualizations are typically different when trying to understand a data phenomenon rather when trying to communicate the insight to stakeholders.

.3 Exploratory Data Analysis Findings

Findings and decisions from EDA require the right packaging when insights are shared with stakeholders. The findings are summarized in a way that the actions taken to clean the data, as well as resulting business insights, can be articulated with appropriate justifications. Analysts validate the results by applying other business analysis techniques such as business rule analysis, process analysis, and elicitation to corroborate the findings from EDA. The EDA scheme, underlying assumptions during EDA, each of the decision points, and the data sourcing process may be communicated along with the business insights.

3.11.4 Usage Considerations

.1 Strengths

- Integrates a visual and intuitive approach to understanding data in a more scientific way.
- Refines the research problem by providing business insights and capturing most of the assumptions related to data upfront.
- Aids in sourcing the right data for a research problem.
- Improves stakeholder confidence that the analytics effort is going in the right direction by providing preliminary findings visually and improves stakeholder engagement.
- Prepares the data for more formal analysis by staging and transforming data before it is used, which increases the performance of the future models.

.2 Limitations

- Often limits the analysis to purely quantitative and statistical intuitions. Analysts may get caught up in analyzing existing data and disregard the bigger picture.
- Usually requires scientific software and analytics platforms. Knowledge of specific programming languages such as R, Python, and associated packages like pandas, SciPy, and seaborn are needed to perform EDA exercises in a meaningful way.
- Models built on the EDA assumptions are not always scalable if the business environment and underlying goals change significantly. A fresh analytics engagement and EDA exercise may be required.

3.12 Hypothesis Formulation and Testing

3.12.1 Purpose

Hypothesis formulation and testing is used in business decision-making where business hypotheses are formulated in a rigorous manner to avoid purely empirical decisions. It is primarily used in problem analysis to transform intuitive assessments to a verifiable and measurable assessment or a research problem.

3.12.2 Description

Hypothesis formulation and testing provides a scientific way to verify hunches, intuition, and experience-based decisions.

Hypothesis testing is also useful when data captured is limited to only a subset or sample of the whole population. For example, a survey may be conducted on a limited number of customers to assess the net promoter score (NPS). The NPS of this sample may not be completely accurate for the entire customer base. Hypothesis testing is used to assign a confidence interval (for example, 95% or 99%) through which a likelihood of the result being correct can be established.

Many variants of hypothesis tests exist, such as t-test, z-test, F-test, and chi square test, which are selected depending upon the circumstance. While the statistical background for each of these types can be reviewed through business statistics textbooks, the primary skill set for an analyst utilizing these techniques is in the formulation of a hypothesis based on the business context and the resulting inference the hypothesis test provides. A data team conducts these tests and the test results are shared with stakeholders.

The following topics are useful in understanding and interpreting the results of hypothesis testing:

- Standardized population and test statistics and their distributions (for example, normal, t, chi square distributions, and the standardized probabilities).
- Central limit theorem and its application in statistics.
- One-tailed and two-tailed tests and associated type I and II errors.

The following table outlines the formulation of the hypothesis:

Scenario	Hypothesis Formulation	Type of Test	Analysis
A bank executive has gathered survey data on 100 customers and observed that average weekly visits are 4.5 per customer with a standard deviation of 2. It indicates that every customer is visiting around 4.5 times a week to the bank. However, the banker believes that the average visit is greater than 5 based on his experience and that the survey is not accurate. A separate study recommends closing 50% of teller windows if weekly average visits are less than 5 to reduce cost.	Null Hypothesis. H_0: The average weekly visit is greater than 5. (H_0: $\mu > 5$)	Lower-tailed z test. Significance level is assumed to be at 5% and computed sample standard deviation is 2. Standard error= 2/ $\sqrt{100}$ = 0.2 Computed z statistic = 4.5-5/0.2=-2.5 At 5% significance (or 95% confidence level) the z score is -1.65 which is greater than -2.5. Hence the null hypothesis can be rejected.	This z-test indicates that the banker's assumptions that there are more visits per week is statistically not sound. The recommendation of closing 50% teller window should not be considered. Analysts could utilize this z-test result to look for more information. For example, the banker may be thinking about pay days when the visits are generally higher.

3.12.3 Elements

.1 Hypothesis Testing Process

Formal hypothesis testing is a statistical process aiding decision-making, refining the research question, and determining whether a variable is a good predictor of the result. For example, an organization might be interested in understanding the impact of Twitter impressions about a product has on the overall sales. Hypothesis testing can be effective in stating that within a certain level of confidence (95%, 97.5% or 99%) it can be statistically tested whether Twitter impressions are a good predictor of sales or not.

The process can be simplified as follows:

1. State the hypothesis.
2. Select appropriate test statistics.
3. Specify the level of significance.
4. State the decision rule regarding the hypothesis.
5. Collect samples and calculate the sample statistics.
6. Make a decision regarding the hypothesis.
7. Provide insights based on the results of the test.

.2 Hypothesis Testing Terminologies

A simple understanding of the terms used in hypothesis testing helps business analysis professionals better collaborate with data analysts and improve the interpretation and communication of the results to the business stakeholders. Some of the common terms include:

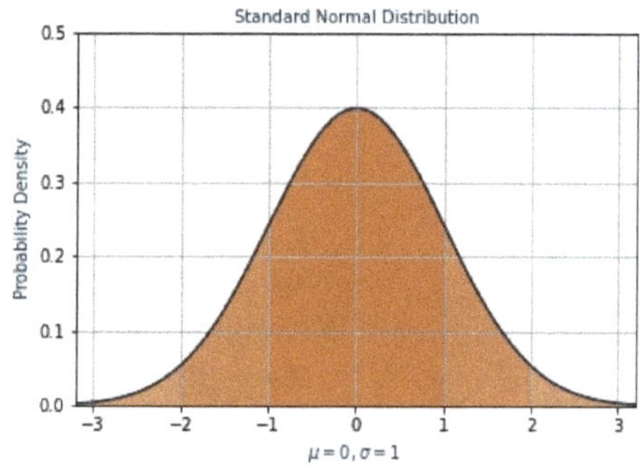

- ***(Standard) Normal distribution:*** The most common type of probability distribution studied. It is a representation of all possible values a variable can take along with its probabilities of occurrence. The mean of this distribution is set to zero by scaling and shifting the mean to zero for easy computation and comparison.
- ***Z score***: Represents the transformed value of a variable scaled down with the standard deviation. For example, the regulation length of a baseball bat is 42 inches (for example, the true/ population mean). A randomly picked bat from a manufacturer measured to 44 inches and the manufacturer has observed a standard deviation of 5 inches. Then z score is

  $$\frac{x_i-\mu}{\sigma} = \frac{44-42}{5} = 0.4\ ,\ \mu = \textit{Mean and}\ \sigma = \textit{Standard deviation.}$$

  That is, in the normal distribution graph this observation is on 0.4σ to the right of the mean at 0.
- ***Level of Significance and Confidence Interval***: It is observed that if a variable follows a normal distribution then almost 95% of observed data (for example, values a variable can take) is between 1.96 σ to -1.96 σ from the mean. From the baseball bat example, there is a 95% probability that any random bat chosen will have the length between (42-1.96x5, 42+1.96x5) inches. Conversely, there are 5% of significant values which are outside this range.
- ***Standard Error of the Mean***: When a sample is taken and the standard deviation is computed, the sample standard deviation overestimates the population standard deviation. That is, the standard deviation of a sample is usually greater than the true standard deviation. Standard error approximates the true standard deviation by correcting this error by dividing the square root of the number of observations in that sample.
- ***Null and Alternate Hypothesis***: The null hypothesis is the default position of a claim that results in no change of the current state. Null hypothesis is denoted as H_0. Alternate hypothesis is the negation of the default position. In the baseball bat example, the manufacturer says the size of

the baseball bats produced is on an average 42 inches. Then the statement can be expressed as $H_0 = 42$, $H_1 \neq 42$. H_A or H_1 represents the alternate hypothesis. The null hypothesis can be rejected or not rejected using a z test.

- ***One-tailed test***: At times analysts are only concerned about observing something which is only one side of the normal curve. For example, an official game cannot take place if the baseball bat length is more than 42 inches. Then significant values are only to the right of the mean. That is $H_0 \leq 42 \text{ and } H_1 > 42$. This type of test would have a 5% significant region to the right of the mean with a 95% confidence level. This is called a one-tailed test.

The explanations of the terminologies are only presented for understanding the background of hypothesis testing. The descriptions are neither comprehensive nor exhaustive. Refer to a business statistics textbook for more details.

3.12.4 Usage Considerations

.1 Strengths

- Hypothesis formulation focuses analysis to a specific business phenomenon or a business problem without drifting into secondary details.
- It aids data collection by limiting the amount of data truly needed to verify a claim.
- With correct formulation of the hypothesis test, variables do not need to follow the restrictions of behaving according to normal distribution. That is, even with fewer assumptions about the underlying factors, a hypothesis test can be performed to verify an outcome.
- Advanced usage such as f score, p values can indicate the factors (variables or combinations) that can together influence a business outcome. A chi square test may be used to compare variances.
- The results from hypothesis tests can be used for further elicitation that aids decision-making.

.2 Limitations

- Hypothesis tests provide the notion of whether a claim is statistically sound or not. It is not a replacement for any analysis led conclusions or decisions through other approaches.
- Using hypothesis tests to establish a claim may ignore data signals which may be uncovered by other means such as exploratory analysis.
- The process and the results may be difficult to communicate to stakeholders. It is advisable for analysts to use simple examples to communicate how hypothesis tests work to build stakeholder confidence.
- Hypothesis testing contains errors which are probabilistic in nature. That is to say that the results do not indicate certainty of outcome. Confidence intervals with appropriate significance levels (for example, threshold values) must be included while stating the outcome of a test.

3.13 Interface Analysis

3.13.1 Purpose

Interface analysis is used to identify where, what, why, when, how, and for whom information is exchanged between solution components or across solution boundaries.

For more information, see *BABOK® Guide* v3, chapter 10.24.

3.13.2 Business Data Analytics Perspective

An interface represents a connection that facilitates the exchange of information between one or more solution components, organizational units, or business processes. Interface analysis helps the team understand what information is exchanged through the interface, as well as the volume of data through that interface.

.1 Identify the Research Question

Interface Analysis does not have a significant role in the Identify the Research Question domain. However, understanding what data is available through different interfaces can be used to frame better quality research questions.

.2 Source Data

During data sourcing, an interface can be analyzed to correlate interface elements to database attributes and discover any underlying data or business rules. How the data is saved in the corresponding database entities can be viewed and these findings can be documented through data mapping to be leveraged during extract, load, and then transform (ELT) activities.

For instance, an update to a customer's profile may update the corresponding data record for the customer, or it may create a new record with an identifier for it being the most recent record. This data mapping work is a beneficial resource for stakeholders who are responsible for business reporting.

.3 Analyze Data

Understanding data transitioned through an interface is important in ensuring good quality data is being generated to answer research questions. Typically, data entered in a system is leveraged for reporting. However, a system acts on that data and generates transactional data which is also valuable to the analytics team.

For instance, to evaluate the success and usage of a newly launched claims application, the analytics team analyzes the data related to the interface to:

- ensure that the interface elements and sequence accurately represent the business process.

- evaluate whether data entered via the interface is being saved in the corresponding entities correctly.
- determine both user and system usage patterns based on activities occurred or events generated. The analysis and reporting of this data helps answer questions such as: What were the most frequently used features in the application? What were the top reasons for an incomplete claim?
- assess system performance and identify top areas of improvement based on system issues. Analysis and reporting of this data helps answer questions related to interface performance such as: What was the average time to complete a claim? What were the top issues with interface usage (for example, time taken to load a page, issue with password entries)? Were there any security issues?

.4 Interpret and Report Results

Interface Analysis does not have a significant role in the Interpret and Report Results domain. However, thoroughly understanding the data generated through various interfaces improves the team's knowledge of how the data is modified, transitioned, and used. This leads to more accurate interpretation and reporting of results.

.5 Use Results to Influence Business Decision-Making

Interface Analysis does not have a significant role in the Use Results to Influence Business Decision-Making domain. However, a thorough understanding of data generated through various interfaces instills confidence in the results and leads to more confidence in influencing decision-making.

.6 Guide Organization-Level Strategy for Business Analytics

Interface Analysis does not have a significant role in the Guide Organization-Level Strategy for Business Analytics domain. However, a good understanding of an organization's interfaces and the data that is generated leads to more robust information and data models that are maintained for organizational use.

3.14 Optimization

3.14.1 Purpose

Business decisions are often based on some amount of uncertainty regarding the outcome. Optimization can be described as choosing the best possible option among multiple available options under some constraints. Optimization as a technique that allows decision-makers to make an informed decision based on available information while acknowledging specific constraints.

3.14.2 Description

Optimization is used differently based on the type of analytics problem or research question. While most descriptive analysis provides the necessary background for Optimization, it is most useful for problems that are predictive or prescriptive in nature. Optimization can be applied differently to both a low- and a high-uncertainty environment.

Consider an organization trying to create a production plan for two products that generate different levels of profit per unit of sale. There are additional constraints which specify limits on resources and time taken to produce each type of product. An optimization scheme can be used to maximize the profits given all the constraints for each product. Such a problem has low uncertainty because the profit is a direct function of the number of units produced for each product, and the resources and time required to produce them is known with a high degree of certainty. Additionally, the profit is linearly dependent on the number of units of production. These types of decision-making problems can be solved using linear programming, which is an optimization technique that is extensively used in logistics, manufacturing, and project management.

There are other types of problems where the result is not related linearly. For example, overall volatility of a stock portfolio is modelled non-linearly based on the volatility of individual stocks. The decision problem in this scenario is to find the best mix of individual stocks (for example, stock weights in a portfolio) with the lowest volatility (for example, risk).

Most machine learning and deep learning applications have a high degree of uncertainty and utilize optimization of some kind. These models try to discover an approximate solution (formally called functional approximation), that best match the available data. The "best match" means that the error is minimized to as low as possible, which indicates an optimization problem. The difference in application of optimization in such scenarios is that an optimum value is found iteratively based on an optimization scheme, such as Laplace's method or gradient descent method, that are very popular in methods for neural networks.

When using Optimization, analysts consider:

Observations regarding optimization	Business analysis perspective
Most analytics problems use optimization in the context of predictive or prescriptive analytics. There are different conventions used by data science professionals to refer to this process, for example, parameter and hyper-parameter tuning, weights optimization, cost/reward function optimization, and so on.	Knowledge of how optimization is used in different problem types help analysts relate to how analytics models are developed.
Most optimization problems lead to an approximate solution or prediction.	Analysts ground the expectations of stakeholders to a reasonable level by explaining how optimization works.
The process of optimization takes time; this is the phase where data science professionals spend most of their time improving analytics models.	Analysts gain a basic understanding of what is being optimized and how, so that the process can be clearly communicated to stakeholders.
Simple problems, such as optimization under low uncertainty, can be quickly computed and analyzed even through basic tools.	Using simple demonstrations tools, such as Excel Solver, help explain and build stakeholder confidence on how optimization can be used. Simple optimization methods are often the most effective supplement the decision-making process.

3.14.3 Elements

.1 Decision Variables

Decision variables are the elements in a decision process that the decision-maker controls. To explain, assume a company produces two garment cleaning products: soap pods and detergent packs. The basic ingredients for the soap pod and the detergent pack are the same but used in different quantities. The cost per unit, as well as time taken to produce, is different for both the products. The decision for decision-makers is to create a production plan which maximizes profit, assuming all produced units are going to be sold.

The elements in control of the decision-makers are how many units of soap pods and detergent packs to produce. These two variables are the decision variables.

When machine learning and related fields are used to generate an analytical model, it is important to note that the predictor variables represent decision variables. The influence of the predictor variables over the outcome (for example, the coefficients/weights in a regression equation) is optimized so that the resulting error is reduced.

.2 Decision/Objective/Cost/Error Function

The decision function represents the goal for the organization and decision-makers. Based on its application, it is referred to as objective, cost, or error function. It can be stated as a mathematical function to succinctly define the relationship between the decision variables and the objective.

Expanding the example of the production plan:

Profit per unit for the soap pod: 20 cents.

Profit per unit for the detergent pack: 50 cents.

Decision variables are:

Number of soap pods to produce: S.

Number detergent packs to produce: D.

Then the objective function that needs to be maximized is:

Profit (\$) = 0.2xS + 0.5xD.

This represents a simple linear programing decision function. Depending on the context, decision functions can be quite complex. Analysts collaborate with the data team to articulate the decision functions clearly to stakeholders and explain how an analytics model works in simple terms.

.3 Constraints

Constraints are the limitations placed on the decision. Analysts help in identifying constraints through a discovery process such as stakeholder elicitation or business rules.

For example, in the production plan problem, the constraints can be that the available labour for the organization is limited to 800 hours. The ingredient for production for both soap pods and detergent packs requires an enzyme and an ethanol, with 20 liters of each available. One detergent pack uses 0.0008 liters of enzyme and 0.0005 of ethanol whereas one soap pod packet uses 0.00001 and 0.0001 liters respectively. The other constraints to note could be that soap pods and detergent packs can be produced only in whole numbers. There may be constraints based on time of manufacturing as well, which may be discovered through further analysis.

.4 Optimization Model

The optimization model is the formulation of decision variables, objective function, and the constraints to a form (usually a mathematical model) so that tools can utilize this information to determine the optimum parameters. The optimization model for the production plan example could be as follows:

Maximize Profit ($) = 0.2 * S + 0.5 * D

Constraints:

0.0008 * D + 0.00001 * S <= 20 liters of enzyme

0.0005 * D + 0.0001 * S <=20 liters of ethanol

S, D are non-negative integer valued

Such a problem can be easily solved using any optimization tool, and complex analytics models use significantly more involved procedures. Analysts collaborate with data science professionals and articulate the analytics model and optimization process to stakeholders.

3.14.4 Usage Considerations

.1 Strengths

- Optimization is the mathematical basis of most of the predictive, prescriptive, and operation research analytical models. Analysts utilize Optimization for a variety of use cases by formulating decision variables, objective function, and the constraints correctly. Some techniques such as linear programming have been in use for a long time and are well accepted for business decision-making.
- Optimization methods converge rapidly (equating to finding the optimum solutions faster) when applied to large scale and complex problems using many variables.

.2 Limitations

- The optimized solution may not be the best solution available (for example, the exact solution).
- More complex formulations are difficult to explain to the stakeholders.
- The process requires very accurate formulation of the constraints. Analysts follow good discovery analysis techniques to uncover any implicit constraints.
- The optimization process in large scale neural networks or large data sets requires processing power and time. It is an iterative process; incorrect formulations often result in time and resource wastage. The data team must collaborate closely to mitigate such risks.

3.15 Problem Shaping and Reframing

3.15.1 Purpose

Problem shaping and reframing are creative applications of problem analysis techniques that result in alternative formulation of the problem faced by an organization. Problem shaping specifically requires refining the problem to a state where a solution process can be applied. Problem reframing refers to re-stating the problem in a different context. Both techniques are interdependent and allow deeper problem analysis leading to simpler or more creative solutions to the problem.

3.15.2 Description

When conducting data related investigation and analysis, there may be a predisposition to review the available data without giving enough attention to the problem. The process followed by data analytics teams may be scientific, comprehensive, and technologically advanced, but may not validate whether the right business problem is being solved. Problem reshaping and reframing helps in understanding the problem from different viewpoints and contexts so that the real business problem or more concrete sub-problems can be uncovered.

Many root cause analysis techniques used during problem analysis are reductive in nature, for example 5 Whys and Fishbone (Ishikawa). These elaborate the business context in which the techniques should be applied, while iteratively developing a detailed understanding of the underlying causes. While such analysis is useful to narrow down the problem, a completely alternate framing of the problem may enable better or easier solutions.

Both problem shaping and reframing require the application of critical thinking and logical deductions that are best explained through examples. Consider a health insurer trying to fix the premium amount for health insurance products:

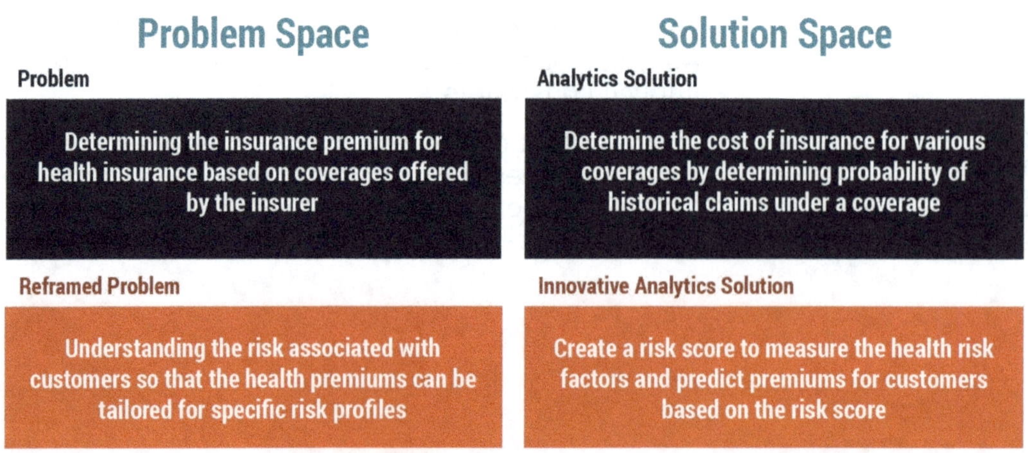

Reframing a problem through a change in the context in which the problem is studied often leads to an alternate understanding of the problem and additional new ways to solve it. In this example, changing the perspective from how the insurer views the problem, to considering the customer perspective that includes the customer lifestyle, demographics, medical history, and so forth.

3.15.3 Elements

.1 Problem Frame and Context

Context refers to the circumstances that influence, are influenced by, and provide understanding of the problem or the solution. The problem is typically analyzed within a context of industry, perceptions, assumptions, best practices, processes, goals, regulations, and any other element that influences the problem or the solution.

When shaping a problem, context is analyzed with additional focus on the problem's symptoms, root causes, constraints, risks, and so on. The underlying context is consciously challenged for problem reframing. As a result, assumptions, perceptions, and business goals may need to be restated.

.2 Problem Statement

The original problem, reshaped problem, or reframed problem is clearly stated and documented. A well-documented problem eliminates any ambiguity in stakeholder perception of the problem and allows focus on the real problem. The problem statement ensures that enough ownership is attributed to respective stakeholders affected by the problem.

A typical reframed or reshaped problem statement may be formed in the following way:

- ***Problem statement***: key statements describing the problem or the opportunity.
- ***Impacted stakeholders***: stakeholders impacted or influenced by the problem.
- ***High level description of the solution or key needs***: for a business data analytics problem, it may contain the analytics approach, required data, and the type of analytics problem (for example, descriptive, predictive, or prescriptive).
- ***Comparison to an alternative formulation of the problem***.

3.15.4 Usage Considerations

.1 Strengths

- Provides a robust analysis of the problem context so that business data analytics engagements are aligned to business objectives.
- Provides an outsider view of the problem, which attracts new and fresh solution approaches.
- Can uncover new data sources that may be needed for analysis.
- Can uncover non-analytics solutions to the problem, which might be simpler or more feasible.

.2 Limitations

- It can create potential conflicts with stakeholder perception of the problem. It is crucial that the data analytics team gets buy-in from key stakeholders.
- It is limited to individual creativity and knowledge while reshaping or reframing the problem. This can be addressed by conducting a group exercise, preferably through brainstorming sessions or stakeholder workshops.
- It may ignore the data cues from previous analysis or introduce the personal bias of influential stakeholder.

3.16 Stakeholder List, Map, or Personas

3.16.1 Purpose

Stakeholder List, Map, Personas assists the team in analyzing stakeholders and their characteristics. From a business data analytics perspective, this technique can be used to understand how stakeholders consume and generate data so that the business data analytics outcomes are aligned to their needs.

For more information, see *BABOK® Guide* v3, chapter 10.43.

3.16.2 Business Data Analytics Perspective

Stakeholder analysis tools are highly beneficial in ensuring proactive and effective communication and engagement with stakeholders during a data initiative. Stakeholder analysis includes:

- Identifying all stakeholders that have a relationship to the data initiative in some capacity.
- Developing understanding of diverse needs, conflicting perspectives, vested interests, and underlying biases to help facilitate conversations towards a shared goal.

- Knowing each stakeholder's knowledge of data analytics.
- Customizing communication methods across different stakeholders or stakeholder groups by ensuring that the right information and right level of information is shared at the right time through the most effective communication channels.
- Determining involvement in various engagements depending on their background, expertise, and vested interests.

Listing and outlining each stakeholder and stakeholder group with pertinent communication details helps the team determine how best to communicate and engage stakeholders.

.1 Identifying the Research Question

The team works with key stakeholders to accurately define the business problem or opportunity. Identifying impacted stakeholders and their implicit and explicit needs is a precursor to this work. Understanding stakeholders' perspective of the current state, their vested interests, and inherent biases, as well as their knowledge of data analytics provides a holistic and deeper understanding of the context.

Stakeholder analysis provides the team with important information, particularly when facilitating a diverse set of stakeholders with conflicting needs. Documenting this information within stakeholder lists, maps, or personas also prove beneficial in subsequent domains when stakeholder communication and engagement needs to be expertly executed.

This work provides a strong foundation for identifying and formulating high quality questions that will be answered through the data analytics effort.

.2 Source Data

In data initiatives that span multiple functional units, there may be a diverse set of data sources and tools leveraged that will then need to be integrated into a single solution. As part of assessing current state, the analytics team identifies how stakeholders consume and generate data using Stakeholder List, Map, and Personas. These consumption patterns help identify the form and function of the data that is utilized in the analytics initiative.

.3 Analyze Data

Descriptive and diagnostic analyses are valuable in revealing what has happened in the past and why. They also provide clues of future trends if the context remains stable. Predictive and prescriptive analyses are highly influential and powerful for decision-making as they reveal possible trends and outcomes that may result under diverse situations, sets of conditions, or alternate decision paths. Stakeholder List, Map, or Personas is used to ensure the analysis work is focused on the topics and issues that are most important to key stakeholders, while aligning with the goals of this work.

.4 Interpret and Report Results

Stakeholder List, Map, or Personas helps the team plan and determine communication strategies for key stakeholders. While the key messages and insights remain the same, there are various factors to consider including:

- ***Preferred type of communication***: Do stakeholders prefer in-person presentations where constructive discussions can take place? Is more passive communication preferred, for example, dashboards accessible online?
- ***Information to be included and the level of detail***: Thought is given to what information should be included. For example, the narrative in a dashboard for a senior executive team may be limited to key highlights and insights, while for a business team there might be more detailed rationale for the results.
- ***Type of visualization***: It is important to identify the most appropriate visuals for the intended audience depending on their comfort level. The use of rich visuals is recommended, but some visuals may be highly technical or perceived complicated for certain audiences.
- ***Formality***: Some stakeholders may prefer results are shared as less structured with a less formal tone, while others may prefer a more formal tone with a structured meeting format to review important insights.
- ***Timing and the frequency of communication***: Timing depends on the urgency of need for the data results. Frequency depends on the purpose for data tracking. Understanding stakeholders helps the team determine the right balance for sharing insights.

.5 Use Results to Influence Business Decision-Making

The analytics team understands the business challenge to be addressed, forms quality research questions, consolidates the appropriate source data, analyzes the data, interprets the results of that analysis to create important insights, and reports their findings. However, their work is not yet complete. The final goal is to see those insights and their evidence-based recommendations used to support business decision-making.

Understanding key stakeholders using Stakeholder List, Map, or Personas increases the probability that the team's recommendations are used responsibly and productively. If the results reveal a clear pattern, and insights are backed by data-based evidence, conclusive recommendations can be made. On the other hand, where no definitive patterns were identified or insights were inconclusive or contrary to what was expected, a consensus needs to be reached on how to move forward. The type of analysis used to draw key insights and how the results are communicated have an influence on the decisions made by stakeholders.

.6 Guide Organization-Level Strategy for Business Analytics

Stakeholder List, Map, or Personas does not have a significant role in the Guide Organization-Level Strategy for Business Analytics domain. However, completing stakeholder analysis helps the analytics team navigate organizational needs for data and information.

3.17 Survey and Questionnaire

3.17.1 Purpose

A survey or questionnaire is used to elicit information including information about customers, products, work practices, and attitudes from a group of people in a structured way and in a relatively short period of time.

For more information, see *BABOK® Guide v3*, Chapter 10.45.

3.17.2 Business Data Analytics Perspective

Surveys and questionnaires can be used to elicit a great deal of information in a relatively short period of time. The design of the questions can dramatically influence the elicited data. Analysts on the data team help structure surveys, questionnaires, and individual questions to ensure quality responses are received.

- ***Identify the research question***: Surveys and questionnaires may be used when exploring the research questions. Results are used to validate if the right questions are being asked, ensuring that the research questions will help the desired outcomes. Both survey design and developing good quality questions to support the overall research questions are critical skills for analysts in a business data analytics context.
  Good question design practices include:
  - understanding the key hypothesis to be tested,
  - developing short questions,
  - utilizing customer ethnography principles,
  - being sensitive to customer sensitivities,
  - aligning questions with overall themes, and
  - ensuring anonymity for respondents.
- ***Source data***: Surveys and questionnaires are popular techniques for actively collecting data. The structure, format, duration, type, and quality of questions, as well as the sample group, are some of the key factors to consider in ensuring the effectiveness of surveys. Skills in statistical sampling methods help achieve unbiased results.
- ***Analyze data***: Data quality concerns or anomalies in the survey results are identified during data analysis. Response rates are carefully monitored to ensure statistical significance. Depending on the severity of the issue, it may be deemed that the survey will need to be re-done (for example, improve quality of questions) or re-sent (for example, data is no longer relevant or reliable or it portrays data bias).
- ***Interpret and report results***: Collating, summarizing, categorizing, and evaluating results allows important themes to emerge from the data. Meaningful insights are then developed to share with the team. Work is required to restructure the results, if it is being shared with stakeholders.
- ***Use results to influence business decision-making***: Depending on the magnitude of changes, the level of risk, and the impact to stakeholders,

surveys and questionnaires may be used to receive feedback that will be considered in the implementation plan. Considering feedback from impacted stakeholders in the change implementation plan may also lower the negative impact of the change.

- ***Guide organization-level strategy for business analytics***: To implement an organization-level strategy (related to data), a strong understanding of how the various functional units currently operate is important. While the strategy remains unchanged, the execution of the strategy may need to be customized to meet any unique, but vital operations within each functional unit. Surveys and questionnaires can be used during large implementations to determine those unique considerations and identify any additional areas of opportunity.

3.18 Technical Visualizations

3.18.1 Purpose

Technical visualizations are used by data scientists to evolve their analysis that becomes the detailed data for driving insights. They may not be useful for communicating insights to business stakeholders, but technical visualizations deepen the team's understanding.

3.18.2 Description

Technical visualizations are a very specific set of data visualization techniques that are used by data scientists to understand data and drive insights. These visuals demonstrate insights that may be statistical or mathematical in nature, which allow data scientists to determine the optimal analytics approach and confirm modelling assumptions related to different types of analytics models.

Analysts are comfortable with common technical visualizations and understand the analysis performed by data scientists. They also simplify, translate, and communicate the impact of certain modelling assumptions or insights with stakeholders. While business visualizations mostly focus on one simplified message or impact related to the business, technical visualizations are focused on discerning data patterns.

3.18.3 Elements

The elements of each technical visualization differ based on the nature of the visualization. A common set of technical visualizations is presented here to demonstrate various technical visuals.

.1 Autocorrelation Plots (Box-Jenkins method)

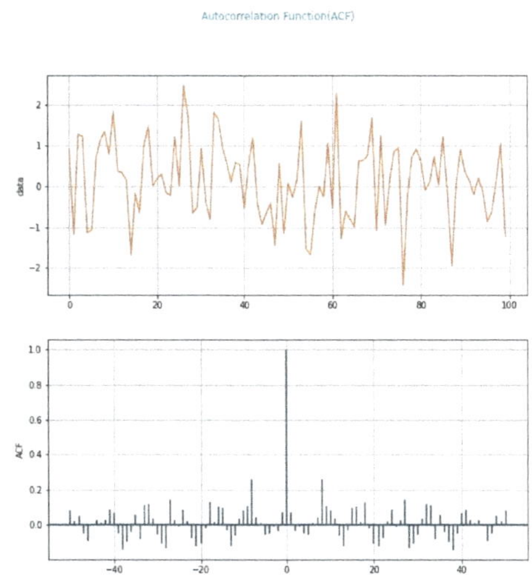

Auto-correlation plots investigate if outcomes are correlated to their historical values. They are especially important in time series analysis. Technically, the plot investigates the correlation of a function with the copy of the function from past periods.

Analysts may infer if the data generated for a time dependent distribution is dependent on its past values from an auto-correlation plot. The data randomly take a value if autocorrelation tends to zero. The top graph is an example of a series of values over time and the bottom graph shows that there is a periodicity in how data behaves over time. Some of the common usages are understanding seasonality in data or examining stock prices and volatility.

.2 Box-Cox Plots/Normal Transformation

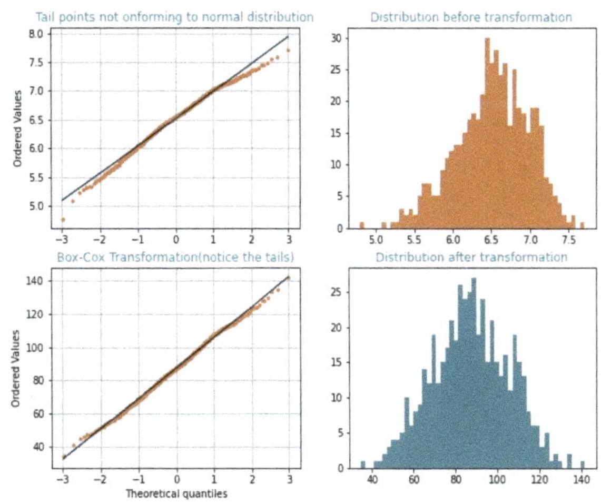

Many analytics models assume that the distribution of a predictor variable follows a normal distribution. Many models that have too much emphasis on sample data do not perform well when applied to new data. Based on context, data scientists may choose to rescale heavily skewed distributions (for example, distributions that are not symmetrical).

For example, some analytics problems require studying recommendations for a restaurant based on the number of reviews and star ratings. It is observed that many of the restaurants have a low number of reviewers. If there are 1 to 20 reviews for many restaurants and 2000 reviews for a few restaurants, the distribution of reviews is skewed. The data scientist may take an approach to remove these outliers (for example, 2000 reviews), but this may not be consistent with the business context. More reviews may mean a higher level of confidence that the restaurants' reviews are valid. In such cases the distribution requires a normal transformation.

Analysts understand and propose the use of transformations based on the context of the problem.

.3 Contour Plots

Visualizing three-dimensional data is difficult. For example, colour coding is one method used if one of the variables takes a list of values represented by the colours. But if the variables take continuous values, visualizations are not adequate in explaining many properties. A contour map transposes the variable to a two-dimensional map with various levels of the third dimension presented as lines or rings.

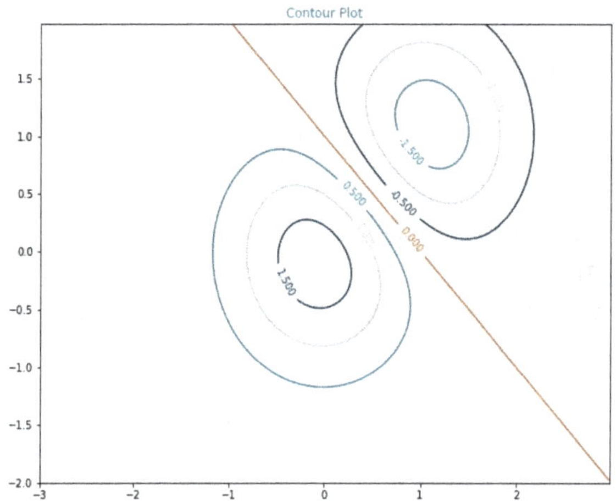

Contour maps are inspired from seismic data analysis. They can explain multiple aspects such as where the data density is high, exploring minimization or maximization problems, deep learning error functions, and gradient analysis.

.4 Correlation Map

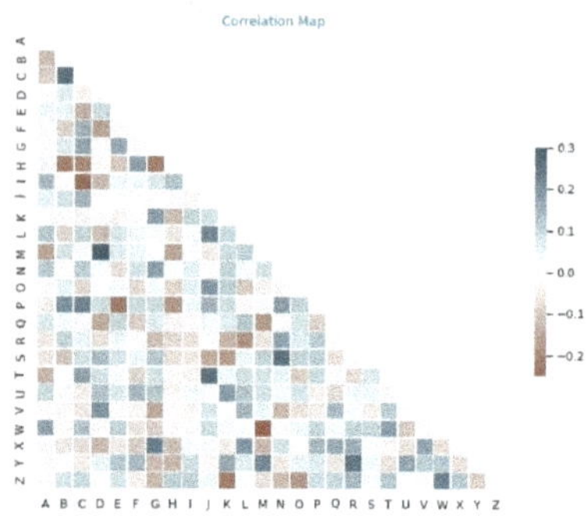

Correlation maps show pairwise correlations between two variables. In many analytics problems, the input data needs to be independent. For example, if a problem is about attrition analysis, there may be two variables that influence the probability of attrition, such as years of experience in an organization and the designation. If these two variables are considered two separate factors the probability is influenced by a combined, rather than the correct. Correlation maps describe this linear dependence by a number between -1 to 1.

p - value is the probability of observing a given data distribution or statistical result purely by chance when the null hypothesis is correct.

Correlation maps are used heavily in analytics problems where models are built under the assumption of variable independence along with key statistical measures (for example, p values) to remove unwanted variables or features from a model.

.5 Principal Component Analysis (PCA) Plot

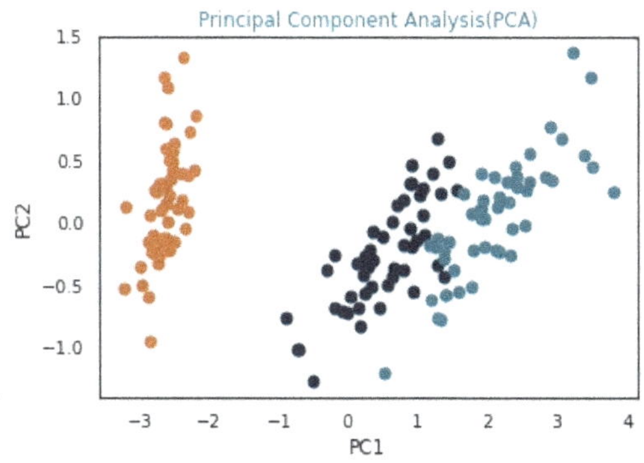

When multiple dimensions of data are involved in producing analytics results, the analytics models start to disintegrate. For example, the loss of predictive power of an analytics model. Current algorithms are quite capable of handling a few hundred variables but problems such as image or video processing generate variables with an order of magnitude that is far more than some algorithms can handle. For example, images are converted to pixels and each pixel reference may serve as a variable. Principal components are programmatically generated to simplify variables which impact the output variable the most.

Consider the following: the analytics problem refers to calculating the blue book value of a used car. The variables or predictors used to estimate the price of the car can include the manufacturer, model, colour, engine rating, number of doors, mileage, and odometer reading, where each can take on different values. Principal components (for example, referred as PC1, PC2 in the illustration) can be different groupings of cars with a similar range of values across these variables. PC1 represents a grouping that has the following characteristic: large engine, high fuel expenditure, high power, and PC2 is its converse. There are 3 distinct categories of cars to focus the analysis on. This pattern is difficult to visualize if all the variables had been considered. By grouping based on principal components, the problem can be solved more efficiently, faster, and with fewer resources.

Analysts are often required to interpret these principal components in business terms to communicate to stakeholders how the analytics model is built. For example, in clustering and market segmentation problems the principal components may describe different customer segments.

.6 Residual Plots

When linear models are used for predictions (for example. linear regression), the expected and actual values of the outcome may differ. The error produced may be plotted against a threshold value to analyze if there are any patterns to the errors. Specific patterns may indicate the goodness of the fitted analytical model. For example, analysts may infer that there is a non-linear relationship present for the output and the data (for example, inverted U in the image).

Heteroskedasticity refers to having error residuals that do not have a constant variance. It indicates that the data behaves differently across different ranges of values.

Hyperparameters of an analytical model or algorithm refers to the parameters that can be controlled to produce different results or control the learning process.

Similarly, some residual plots may indicate heteroskedasticity (for example, indicative of subgroups within data with different attributes), which may change the nature of the models used.

Similarly, analytical modelling parameters can be tuned (for example, hyperparameter tuning) by reviewing cumulative error plots for different hyperparameter combinations.

.7 Receiver Operating Characteristics (ROC) Curve

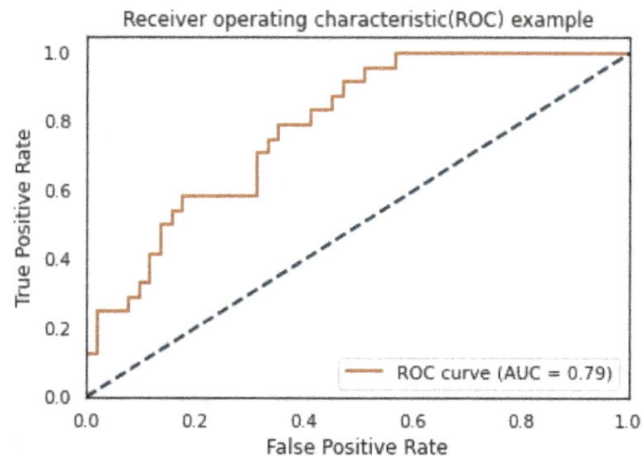

In many classification problems (for example, fraud detection), there are instances where traditional measures of performance are not adequate. The true positive rate (TPR) and false positive rate (FPR) can be manipulated by using a threshold parameter, thereby changing the evaluation criteria such as accuracy, precision, recall, and so on. This achieves the required level of trade-off between the evaluation parameters that is suitable for the classification problem.

The ROC curve plots the FPR and TPR on XY coordinates in a graph. The more area under the curve (AUC)) based on threshold values, the better the predictive model it is for a classification research problem.

The ROC may be used for establishing a baseline classifier (for example, classification model) and be compared against different classifiers. This helps data science professionals choose the appropriate algorithm to fine-tune further.

.8 Silhouette Plot

There are many applications of clustering problems in different business contexts, for example, market segmentation, news classification, object detection, crime hotspots detection, and natural language processing. The models developed for these applications are visually verified to ensure that the parameters used, such as number of clusters and the definition of similarity between observations, can produce the right result. The silhouette plot shows the results of clustering in a visual way. One silhouette map can contain a lot of information about the overall clustering model.

A silhouette plot usually depicts different clusters on the Y axis, and the length of silhouettes in the X axis is represented with a metric known as a silhouette score. The score varies between -1 to 1. A clear delineation of a cluster requires the silhouettes to be as wide and as long as possible in the plot.

For example, if the image were to depict different market segments based on customers and their buying patterns, the following insights can be deduced:

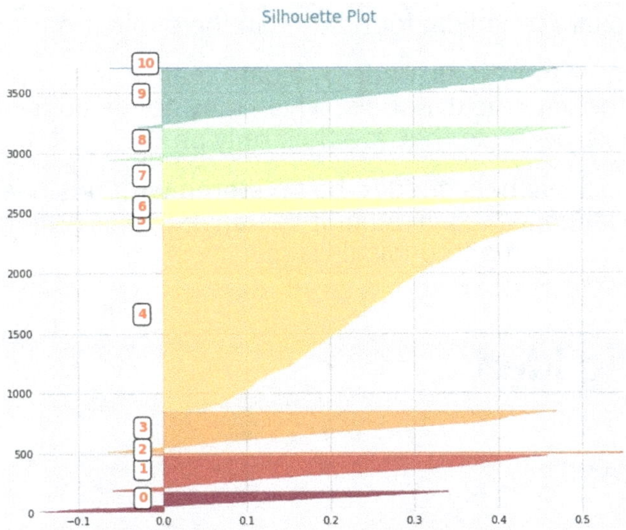

- Although the number of segments chosen is 10, there are only four to five dominant clusters or customer segments. Analysts might reduce the number of clusters in the analytics model.
- The cluster number 4 has a very narrow silhouette compared to its width. This may be reducing the average length of the silhouettes. It may indicate that this cluster could be broken up in to more homogeneous segments.
- There are some clusters with negative starting range. For example, cluster 0, 5. These two clusters also have narrow silhouette. This further suggests that these clusters can be removed from analysis resulting in smaller number of market segment.

3.18.4 Usage Considerations

.1 Strengths

- Collectively, most technical visuals provide insights related to the analysis process, such as model selection, modelling assumptions, and model fits, that increase the performance of analytical models and reduce the time taken to develop these models.
- Most technical visualizations are well-defined and discussed for different types of analytics problems, which allows a systematic analytics approach to be developed.
- Technical visualizations can communicate how and why some of the analytical modelling choices are made. Without visualizations, the rationale for these choices can be lost for stakeholders.
- There are several tools and techniques at the disposal of data science professionals and analysts to create standard visuals.

.2 Limitations

- Interpretation of technical visuals may be challenging without the necessary technical foundation in the subject matter.
- The interpretations made by a data team due to the technical visuals may bias the analytical models, which may not be consistent with the business context, because they are built only on the available data.
- Technical visuals need to be bolstered with business and domain knowledge, which is difficult to translate into empirical rules used in the interpretation of technical visuals

3.19 The Big Idea

3.19.1 Purpose

The "big idea" is a concept that helps analysts communicate an important foundational or central insight to stakeholders. By removing extraneous information, the stakeholders better understand the essence of the key insight.

Effectively communicating the big idea increases the chance of influencing key stakeholders to take a recommended course of action.

3.19.2 Description

The big idea is used to convey an insight, story, or concept in a way that gains attention from stakeholders. The big idea distills an interpretation of an insight or answer to a question into one single, powerful statement of fact that compels key stakeholders to make a decision.

There are three integral parts to a big idea:

- ***Understanding the audience***: Who are the key stakeholders? Who are the decision-makers? Who are the influencers? What are their biases? What is the action been recommended?
- ***Understanding the impact on key stakeholders***: Why should certain stakeholders agree to a specific business decision? What would happen if the recommended action is not followed?
- ***Communicating the big idea***: Communicate a data-driven recommendation that satisfies the business need. Simply stated as a concise statement about what needs to be done and what maybe lost if the recommended is not followed.

The simplicity of the big idea ensures that stakeholders understand what is at stake. The big idea is often used during data presentations, along with the results, narrative, and business visualizations to frame the insights and recommendations.

Using a structured approach helps refine the big idea. The following template is one example:

Big Idea Template

WHO IS YOUR **AUDIENCE?**

1. List the primary groups or individuals to whom you'll be communicating
2. If you had to narrow that to a single person, who would that be?
3. What does your audience care about?
4. What action does your audience need to take?

WHAT IS **AT STAKE?**

What are the benefits if audience acts in the way that you want them to?

What are the risks if they do not?

FORM YOUR **BIG IDEA**

It should:

1. articulate your point of view,
2. convey what's at stake, and
3. be a complete (and single) sentence

Adapted from: Ricks, E. *what toddlers can teach us about data storytelling*. StoryTellingwithData.com. http://www.storytellingwithdata.com/blog/category/Big+Idea. 2020.

3.19.3 Elements

.1 Audience Details (Who is your audience?)

The details of the audience include who is impacted by the analytics outcome or the insight that analysts want to communicate to a specific audience.

Analysts carefully assess if there are stakeholder biases that could impact the recommended action or if there could be conflicts created by the recommendation. Analysts consider what level of influence or impact key stakeholders could have on the recommendation or insight being communicated. Reviewing the stakeholder analysis that was completed during the analytics initiative is a critical component to helping formulate the big idea.

.2 Impact of Change (What is at stake?)

The impact of rejecting the recommended course of action is addressed through the big idea. Negative impact can be widespread and may include impacts to existing processes, future finances, brand value, and even the business model. The impact is explained in a way to that the audience can relate. For example, executive decision-makers may not want to get into system level changes or impact, but will be very interested in the business outcome. The potential impact also includes a discussion of opportunity costs and risks.

.3 The Big Idea Outline

The big idea articulates the primary insight discovered from the analytics effort. The business decision, course of action, or the insight explained through the big idea may be accompanied by an explanation of success. For example, "Tracking success of our marketing campaign" is not the big idea, but "10% increased investment in digital marketing would result in a 40% increase in revenue by end of the next quarter" is. The big idea is fully formed and described in a way that compels action from decision-makers.

3.19.4 Usage Considerations

.1 Strengths

- Provides a direct and declarative statement involving a business decision.
- Reduces ambiguity in interpretation of insights among stakeholders.
- Can be used as a concluding summary for a 3-minute story, a data journey, a business visualization, or an analytics solution demonstration to underline the expected outcome.

.2 Limitations

- The big idea may not be useful if there is a lack of evidence or presence of bias from stakeholders.
- Without proper stakeholder analysis the big idea may lead to conflict.
- Multi-level insights are difficult to communicate through the big idea.

3.20 3-Minute Story

3.20.1 Purpose

A 3-minute story is used to describe certain aspects of an analytics engagement. The explanation can include the intent, key findings, relevant business decision, or a recommendation. It is a natural and concise summary of the intent, analysis, and the outcome being communicated to key stakeholders, from their perspective.

3.20.2 Description

A 3-minute story is a tool that is often used to succinctly communicate a business scenario to stakeholders. The term “3-minute” is a placeholder and a reminder to communicate the message concisely and precisely. The 3-minute stories often contain a key fact or insight that can anchor the attention of stakeholders. This begins with clarity about what will be achieved through the story and also requires the analyst to be aware of the story setting including:

- background and supporting information regarding the narrative,
- knowledge of the stakeholders and their biases,
- factors that are advantageous to the story and factors that could weaken the message of the story, and
- the components of a successful outcome. For example, funding, justification for an insight, business actions, or interventions

The setting of the story is needed for a precise construction of the narrative, and is also useful in answering follow-up questions. The 3-minute story is a consultative tool for communicating data insights, key messages through visuals, or recommendations from analytics engagements, particularly for stakeholders where time is a constraint.

Many business visualizations in an analytics context require analysts to step out of the data and state the message or insights upfront. A 3-minute story is a good tool to accompany business or technical visualizations.

3.20.3 Elements

.1 Intent

The intent of a 3-minute story, in a data analytics context, is to express the purpose for the data narrative or the purpose of the communication. This intent is explained to the upfront. The setting in which a research question is posed explained (for example, different business situations such as decreasing costs, improving marketing effectiveness, or studying operational risks). Analysts provide context of the analysis along with a story hook (a relevant, interesting, or shocking fact) that captures stakeholders' attention.

Keeping it simple and focusing on single questions or story hooks helps maintain focus on the key message of the story.

.2 Analysis

Most high-level actions related to the study of the question or story hook is described in the narrative of the story. Analysts may construct the narrative of a 3-minute story with a set of sequential actions; however, the details of analysis may be restricted to simple statements of facts. The analysis may end with a single, but compelling, finding from the analysis that is relevant to key stakeholders or the business.

.3 Outcome

The outcome of a 3-minute story is simple and clearly stated as an action on the part of stakeholders. For example, it may involve a decision about budget or agreeing on a specific business direction. It is useful to close the 3-minute story with a summary statement, a question for key stakeholders, or prompting a decision to be made.

3.20.4 Usage Considerations

.1 Strengths

- Provides a clear, cohesive, and concise explanation of an analytics outcome.
- Can be used as a tool to express or explain a key message or theme. This is especially useful in executive communications or influencing decision-makers.
- In an analytics context, it complements many visuals to emphasize a key message.
- It can prompt stakeholders to make a decision or approve some other action.

.2 Limitations

- Complex ideas are difficult to communicate through a 3-minute story.
- It does not follow any prescribed format or standard outline.
- 3-minute story is mostly used in combination with other techniques to emphasize the message.

Appendix 4: Bibliography

Articles, White Papers, Podcasts, and Publications

- *Analyzing Quantitative Research*. Center for Innovation in Research and Teaching.
- Berger, C. *Big Data Analytics with Oracle Advanced Analytics*. Oracle. July 2015.
- Berinato, S. *Data Science and the Art of Persuasion.* Harvard Business Review. January 2019.
- Biddix, Dr. J. Patrick. *Writing Research Questions*. ResearchRundowns. July 20, 2009.
- Chibana, N. *Data Storytelling*. Visme.
- Compiled by students in CEP955, Michigan State University. *Qualities of a Good Research Purpose and/or Questions*. SUNY Cortland. 2013.
- *Data Sampling*. SearchBusinessAnalytics. September 2018.
- Devaux, E. *Graph Visualization: Why it Matters*. Linkurious. September 2017.
- Dorris, Martha. *What's Your Strategy? Operational Excellence, Product Leadership or Customer Intimacy?*. DigitalGov. December 2, 2013.
- Dykes, Brent. *Data Storytelling: Data Storytelling - The Essential Data Science Skill Everyone Needs*. Forbes. March 2016
- Enochson, Heyden. *27 Examples of Key Performance Indicators*. OnStrategy. 2018.
- Excel team. *Breaking down hierarchical data with Treemap and Sunburst charts*. August 2015. Microsoft.
- Excel Tips. *A Step-by-step Guide on Creating a BULLET Chart in Excel.* Trump Excel. May 2015.
- *Funnel Chart*. FusionCharts.
- Henke, N., Jordan Levine, and Paul McInerney. *You Don't Have to Be a Data Scientist to Fill This Must-Have Analytics Role.* Harvard Business Review. February 2018.
- Herring, L., Helen Mayhew, Akanksha Midha, and Ankur Puri. *How to Train Someone to Translate Business Problems into Analytics Questions*. February 2019.
- *Introduction to Data Analysis Handbook*. Academy for Educational Development ,2006.
- Kozyrkov, C. *What Great Data Analysts Do - and Why Every Organization Needs Them*. Harvard Business Review. December 2018.
- *MapR Guide to BigData in Telecommunications*. MapR Technologies, Inc. 2017.

- Oetting, J. *Data Visualization 101: How to Choose the Right Chart or Graph for Your Data*. HubSpot. May 2018.
- *Percentiles, Percentile Rank & Percentile Range: Definition & Examples*. Statistics How To. 2019.
- Pratt, M. *Business intelligence vs. business analytics: Where BI fits into your data strategy*. CIO. September 2017.
- Ricks, E. *What toddlers can teach us about data storytelling.* StoryTellingwithData.com http://www.storytellingwithdata.com/blog/category/Big+Idea. 2020.
- Saxena, A. *Why Your Data Strategy Needs to Align with Your Business Strategy*. Dataversity. January 2019.
- Saxena, A. *Data as Storyteller: Three Ways to Turn Your Analytics into Action.* Dataversity. July 2018.
- Saxena, A. *3 Critical Pieces of Data Groundwork for Modern Business Strategy*. CEO Insider. April 2018.
- Statistics Canada. *Constructing box and whisker plots*. www.statcan.gc.ca. October 2017.
- Silverman, Lori. *Business Analysis: Data - An Essential Insight in Driving Transformation & Business Success*. IIBA Podcast. International Institute of Business Analysis. February 2019. https://www.youtube.com/watch?v=VRNcRszqJFA&feature=youtu.be.
- Tejada Z., Marc Wilson, Alex Buck, Mike Wasson. *Advanced Analytics*. Microsoft. February 2018.
- *Tips for data migration after a merger.* ETL Solutions. https://www.etlsolutions.com/new/tips-for-data-migration-after-a-merger/https://www.etlsolutions.com/new/tips-for-data-migration-after-a-merger/.

Reference Books

- Berinato, S. *Good Charts: The HBR Guide to Making Smarter, More Persuasive Data*. Harvard Business Review Press. 2016.
- Cole Nussbaumer Knaflic. *Storytelling with Data: A Data Visualization Guide for Business Professionals*. Wiley. 2018.
- Daniel, W. and James Terrell. *Business Statistics, Basic Concepts and Methodology*. Houghton Mifflin. 1997.
- Davenport, T. H., Harris, J. G., and R. Morison. *Analytics at Work: Smarter decisions, better results*. Harvard Business Press. 2010.
- Dietz, K. and Lori Silverman. *Business Story Telling for Dummies*. Wiley. 2014.
- Harvard Business Review. *HBR Guide to Data Analytics Basics for Managers*. Harvard Review Press. 2019.
- Holsapple, C., A. Lee-Post, and R. Pakath. *A unified foundation for business analytics*. Decision Support Systems Volume 64 Issue C. 2014. 130-141.
- Hubbard, D.W. *How to Measure Anything: Finding the Value of Intangibles in Business*. Wiley. 2014.
- International Institute of Business Analysis. *A Guide to the Business Analysis Body of Knowledge® (BABOK® Guide)*, Version 3. International Institute of Business Analysis. 2015.
- Jones, Herbert. *Data Science for Business: Predictive Modeling, Data Mining, Data Analytics, Data Warehousing, Data Visualization, Regression Analysis, Database Querying, and Machine Learning for Beginners*. Herbert Jones. 2018.

- Laursen, G. H. and J. Thorlund. *Business analytics for managers: Taking business intelligence beyond reporting*. Wiley. 2016.
- Nassbaumer Knaflic. C. *Storytelling with Data*. John Wiley & Sons, Inc. 2015.
- Ogilvy, D. *Ogilvy on Advertising*. Prion Books Ltd. 2007,
- Provost, Foster and Tome Fawcett. D*ata Science for Business: What You Need to Know about Data Mining and Data-Analytic Thinking*. O'Reilly. 2013.
- Saxena, Rahul Narain, and Anand Srinivasan. *Business Analytics: A Practitioner's Guide*. Springer. 2013.
- Shmueli, G., Peter C. Bruce, Inbal Yahav, Nitin R Patel, and Kenneth C Lichtendahl Jr. *Data Mining for Business Analytics: Concepts, Techniques, and Applications*. Wiley. 2017.
- Simon, P. *Too Big to Ignore: The Business Case for Big Data*. Wiley. 2013.
- Siegel, E. *Predictive Analytics: The Power to Predict Who Will Click, Buy, Lie, or Die*. 2013. John Wiley & Sons.
- Viaene, S. and Annabel Van den Bunder. T*he Secrets to Managing Business Analytics Projects*. MIT Sloan Management Review v53. 2011. 65-69.

Appendix 5: Contributors

IIBA would like following community members whose valuable contributions made the Guide To Business Data Analytics possible.

Guide To Business Data Analytics

Authors

- Ananta Mahapatra
- Ashish Mehta
- Aparna Iyer
- Earle Pereira
- Eric Gingrich
- Jas Phul
- Kassem Nasser
- Laura Paton
- Melanie Lee
- Melody Borman Hicks
- Mohamed Zahran
- Opeyemi Adeniran-Oyediran
- Peter Adeniran

Reviewers

- Ali Khater
- Alon Hadass
- Awe Oludayo
- Darcey Leischner
- Georgy Saveliev

- Jiji Curie
- Jennifer Bwamu
- Dr. Mark Griffin
- Markus Lin
- Michal Maroszek
- Natalia Inglezou
- Sohail Sadiq
- Sri Pilla
- Sruti Chandra
- Swaroop Oggu

Introduction To Business Data Analytics (Practitioner and Organizational Views)

Authors

- Anne Tixier
- Laura Paton, MBA, CBAP, IIBA-AAC, CSM (Chair)
- Leelyn Cruddas
- Dr. Mark Griffin

Reviewers

- Angela Weller, CSM, CSPO
- Anna Sloan
- Charlotte DeKeyrel
- Darcey Leischner, CSM
- Jodie Kane, CPBA, CSM, CSPO, CPBI
- JoJo John
- Kunal Joshi, PMP, CBAP
- Melanie Lee, MSc, CBAP, CSPO
- Melody Hicks
- Parvathi Ramesh, CA, CBAP, CISA
- Ramanpal Singh Anand
- Sruti Chandra, MBA, CBAP
- Swaroop Oggu